HOME ON TIME

LIFE MANAGEMENT BY THE BOOK

RYAN RUSH

SPRINGFIELD, MISSOURI 65807

HOME ON TIME

Copyright © 2003 by Life and Family Ministries, Inc., D.B.A. Home On Time
Driftwood, Texas 78619
All rights reserved.

Published by 21st Century Press
Springfield, Missouri U.S.A.
Printed in U.S.A.

21st Century Press is an evangelical Christian publisher dedicated to serving the local church with purpose books. We believe God's vision for 21st Century Press is to provide church leaders with biblical, user-friendly materials that will help them evangelize, disciple and minister to children, youth and families.

It is our prayer that this book will help you discover biblical truth for your own life and help you meet the needs of others. May God richly bless you.

Unless otherwise noted, Scripture quotations in this text are taken from the New King James Version, Copyright © 1979, 1980, 1982 by Thomas Nelson, Inc., Publishers. Used by permission.

All rights reserved. No part of this book may be used or reproduced in any manner whatsoever or stored in any database or retrieval system without written permission except in the case of brief quotations used in critical articles and reviews. Requests for permissions should be addressed to:

21st Century Press
2131 W. Republic Rd.
PMB 41
Springfield, MO 65807
800-658-0284

ISBN: 0-9728899-0-6

Cover: Lee Fredrickson
Book Design: Terry White
Visit our web-site at: 21stcenturypress.com and 21stcenturybooks.com
For great children's books visit: sonshipbooks.com

PUBLISHING WITH PURPOSE
WWW.21STCENTURYPRESS.COM

CONTENTS

BLE Pre-Test 4

BLE Score Sheet 10

BLE Explanation 11

Defining Time 13

Power of Response 27

Power of Direction 55

Power of Planning 87

Power of Action 111

The Greatest News in the Entire Book 141

Family Time Inventory 144

The First Forty Day Test 147

Super Summary 179

BLE Post-Test 181

BLE Score Sheet 187

BLE Explanation 188

Bring a Home On Time Conference to Your Church 190

About the Author 191

DEDICATION

To my family. Your prayers keep me going. Your love and laughter make my life rich.

THE BALANCED LIFE EVALUATION
"PRE-BOOK INVENTORY"

The Balanced Life Evaluation is a tool to help you get the most out of *Home on Time: Life Management By The Book*. By taking a few moments to complete these questions, you can gain a better understanding of what areas in your life need the most attention.

Please answer as accurately as possible. This quiz is more a reflection of yourself than a scientific instrument. You can easily fudge the answers to make yourself feel better, but you will miss out on the opportunity to see a more detailed picture of your life. Remember – you are responding according to what you actually DO, and not how you HOPE to DO in the future. The more honest you are on these questions, the more helpful this exercise can be.

1) I accept the fact that many things in my life are out of my control.
____ 1. Almost Never
____ 2. Seldom
____ 3. Sometimes
____ 4. Most of the Time
____ 5. Almost Always

2) I operate on a personal mission statement I have formulated for my life.
____ 1. Almost Never
____ 2. Seldom
____ 3. Sometimes
____ 4. Most of the Time
____ 5. Almost Always

3) I like to have access to as much information as possible before making a decision.
_____ 1. Almost Never
_____ 2. Seldom
_____ 3. Sometimes
_____ 4. Most of the Time
_____ 5. Almost Always

4) If someone followed me through an average day, he would get a clear picture of the things that matter most to me.
_____ 1. Almost Never
_____ 2. Seldom
_____ 3. Sometimes
_____ 4. Most of the Time
_____ 5. Almost Always

5) When making decisions, I take into account things around me that could affect my plans. (i.e., culture, rules, other people, etc...)
_____ 1. Almost Never
_____ 2. Seldom
_____ 3. Sometimes
_____ 4. Most of the Time
_____ 5. Almost Always

6) By keeping my priorities in mind, I am able to say no to distractions and interruptions throughout my day.
_____ 1. Almost Never
_____ 2. Seldom
_____ 3. Sometimes

_____ 4. Most of the Time
_____ 5. Almost Always

7) When pursuing a goal, I break it down into simple, logical steps.
_____ 1. Almost Never
_____ 2. Seldom
_____ 3. Sometimes
_____ 4. Most of the Time
_____ 5. Almost Always

8) I have a system for easy completion of things I must do on a regular basis, like bill paying, house chores, filing, etc., so that these tasks are more easily completed.
_____ 1. Almost Never
_____ 2. Seldom
_____ 3. Sometimes
_____ 4. Most of the Time
_____ 5. Almost Always

9) I am willing to change my plans in order to accommodate changing circumstances.
_____ 1. Almost Never
_____ 2. Seldom
_____ 3. Sometimes
_____ 4. Most of the Time
_____ 5. Almost Always

10) I avoid things that do not really matter, like television, surfing the Internet, and computer or video games.

____ 1. Almost Never
____ 2. Seldom
____ 3. Sometimes
____ 4. Most of the Time
____ 5. Almost Always

11) I use one planning system for my daily life, whether it is a paper planner or digital handheld device.
____ 1. Almost Never
____ 2. Seldom
____ 3. Sometimes
____ 4. Most of the Time
____ 5. Almost Always

12) My goals have been given a date of completion.
____ 1. Almost Never
____ 2. Seldom
____ 3. Sometimes
____ 4. Most of the Time
____ 5. Almost Always

13) I am comfortable with doing what I ought to do even when I receive little or no immediate rewards in return.
____ 1. Almost Never
____ 2. Seldom
____ 3. Sometimes
____ 4. Most of the Time
____ 5. Almost Always

14) My short and long term goals are clearly written down.
_____ 1. Almost Never
_____ 2. Seldom
_____ 3. Sometimes
_____ 4. Most of the Time
_____ 5. Almost Always

15) I find the information I need quickly, because my system of information storage is in order.
_____ 1. Almost Never
_____ 2. Seldom
_____ 3. Sometimes
_____ 4. Most of the Time
_____ 5. Almost Always

16) When I begin my tasks for the day, I jump right in and get to work.
_____ 1. Almost Never
_____ 2. Seldom
_____ 3. Sometimes
_____ 4. Most of the Time
_____ 5. Almost Always

17) I can often anticipate problems before they arise in the future.
_____ 1. Almost Never
_____ 2. Seldom
_____ 3. Sometimes
_____ 4. Most of the Time
_____ 5. Almost Always

18) I review my short and long-term goals regularly.
   ____ 1. Almost Never
   ____ 2. Seldom
   ____ 3. Sometimes
   ____ 4. Most of the Time
   ____ 5. Almost Always

19) I am on time for my appointments and planned activities.
   ____ 1. Almost Never
   ____ 2. Seldom
   ____ 3. Sometimes
   ____ 4. Most of the Time
   ____ 5. Almost Always

20) I make it a point to stay physically fit and eat healthy foods.
   ____ 1. Almost Never
   ____ 2. Seldom
   ____ 3. Sometimes
   ____ 4. Most of the Time
   ____ 5. Almost Always

Transfer the answers from your Balanced Life Evaluation to the blanks below and to the left. Next, fill in the blank to the right of each answer with the same number. Finally, add up the four columns to discover your scores in each category.

Answers	R	D	P	A
1.	☐			
2.		☐		
3.			☐	
4.				☐
5.	☐			
6.		☐		
7.			☐	
8.				☐
9.	☐			
10.		☐		
11.			☐	
12.				☐
13.	☐			
14.		☐		
15.			☐	
16.				☐
17.	☐			
18.		☐		
19.			☐	
20.				☐
(Add each column)	Response	Direction	Planning	Action
TOTALS	☐	☐	☐	☐

The Balanced Life Evaluation is scored in four critical areas of the productivity process:

> **Response**: the ability to anticipate and respond with wisdom to the out-of-control aspects of life.
>
> **Direction**: the knowledge of how success will be defined in your life and that of your family, and setting the goals to get there.
>
> **Planning**: the organization of tasks and events to line them up with priorities and goals.
>
> **Action**: the demonstration of true commitment to your plans by going forward with the necessary tasks.

Out of a possible 25 points in each category, fill in the points you accumulated in each:

Response: ____
Direction:____
Planning:____
Action: ____

Some numbers to consider:

> A score of 0 – 7 in any category may mean that this area of your life is in desperate need of attention!

> A score of 8 – 12 in any category indicates that there is work to be done to achieve maximum productivity in this area.

> A score of 13 – 18 in any category means that you have obviously developed some positive habits in this area. Be sure that you bring

ALL of your categories up to this level, or this strength could become a weakness.

A score of 19 – 25 means that you are making a consistent effort, and places you in the company of a select few self-disciplined individuals on earth at this time. Use your strengths to make a difference for eternity!

There are two areas of interest you need to focus on with these scores.

LIFE BALANCE:

With regard to balance, you will want to imagine that each of these areas is a weight on one corner of a circle. This circle is balancing on a needle, and will stay balanced only as long as each end weighs the same. If it's out of balance at all, it will have a strong chance of toppling over in the long haul.

The weaker areas need to be improved first in order to improve balance, which will automatically improve productivity.

SCOPE:

With regard to scope, you will want to imagine that the bigger your scores, the bigger the "bulls-eye" on life's target becomes. In other words, you have a much greater chance of accomplishing what's important to you when all four areas have been enlarged.

This self-evaluation can be greatly enhanced by inputting your answers online at www.homeontime.com. Your response will be evaluated, and you can receive a chart which illustrates these important principles. This evaluation is a free service. Take advantage today!

INTRODUCTION

CAUTION: YOU'RE ON THE CLOCK

DEFINING TIME

The average American is traveling through life at warp speed and has no idea of how to slow down, how to regain control, and often with no destination in mind. Sadly, most of us do not even realize how little time we have. Because we have never really taken the time to grasp how to manage our time effectively, we try to rush through life – assuming that speed and quantity of tasks will compensate for quality and sense of accomplishment.

Home On Time: Life Management By the Book is here to help you get the things that matter done in your lifetime. Our basis for the whole concept was derived out of one key passage of Scripture found in the book of Psalms. Psalm 90 is undoubtedly the oldest Psalm in the Bible. The author is

Moses – the great leader who brought the Jews out of Egyptian slavery and whom God used instrumentally in establishing His laws and covenant. This insightful chapter takes a look back into the life of Moses, a look around at the time of the writing and the circumstances involved, and a look ahead at hope for passing on a legacy to future generations. Throughout the chapter, one specific theme holds true – **our perspective of time and the way we put it to use will have a major impact on future success.**

In Psalm 90, God makes one thing clear: He is eternal, and we (at least during our lifetime on earth) are not.

> "¹ A Prayer of Moses the man of God. Lord, You have been our dwelling place in all generations. ² Before the mountains were brought forth, Or ever You had formed the earth and the world, Even from everlasting to everlasting, You are God."

God is eternal, but sooner or later, you are going to die. Now how's that for an encouraging way to begin a book? I just thought I would get the bad news out of the way from the start. Perhaps some more surprising data might be a shock after the first pronouncement: **you have less time to live than you think.** I base that brash statement on two pieces of evidence:

1. While there is no way to ask people if they were surprised at how soon they died, I believe that an informal poll, if it were possible, would yield very solid evidence that people expected to have more time.

Imagine attending a funeral when the preacher says, "Well, thank the Lord he's finally gone. He's been finished with all of his work here on earth for years. Totally content and ready to go." Ever been to one of those? I seriously doubt it. There may be those who pass away who have not accomplished much in years, but that does not mean they did not have more to do that didn't get done.

2. During the time on earth that we are living now, very little of it is actually spent on what I would consider living – those aspects of life that have an eternal impact and bring us joy in living. The following illustration demonstrates why we have so little time to really live. We will start by listing the things in life that we all have to deal with and take up time. Then we will mark down about how much time they take up in the average 24-hour period. These are not national averages – just realistic and conservative estimates for normal people like us.

I'll call them **"The Inevitables"**:

Sleep . . . . .7.5 Hrs.
We're supposed to get eight a night, but who does?

Dress/ Personal Hygiene . . . . .1 Hr.
If you spend less than one hour on this, don't brag about it!

Occupation/ Child Rearing . . . . .6.6 Hrs.
I averaged a 46 hour work week and divided by 7. If you are a full-time mom, then this is probably a low number for the work you do, but it will do

for the analogy.

Commuting ....1 Hr.	
Give or take, but this includes to and from all your destinations.	

Home Maintenance/ Chores/ Paperwork ..5 Hrs.	
Bills, chores, and paperwork take more time than you think.	

Eating..1 Hr.	
I know by looking in the mirror that this is way low for me!	

Shopping/Errands ....5 Hrs.	
For my wife, this is low. But I wanted to have some time remaining on the schedule to work with!	

Total So Far: ....18.1 Hours	

Now, that leaves us with 5.9 hours remaining on the clock. You might be saying, "Wow! I'd love to have six hours to work with on my schedule." Not so fast! Before you get too excited, consider all of the things that you want to fit into that remaining time slot.

Remaining Priorities:

    Time with God
    Family Time
    Mental and Physical Development
    Friendships
    Rest
    _____(whatever your passion in life is)

These are the things that life is really made of. I do not know anybody that says, "I can't wait to get up tomorrow and brush my teeth! I'm so looking forward to getting back in the car for my long drive to work." No – with very few exceptions, we live for the events that do not just happen – playing ball in the backyard with our kids, a great vacation, or an evening with friends. **We look forward to the times that must be *intentionally planned* – the part of life that is really living will not happen by accident.**

Here is another way of looking at these 5.9 hours. If that is roughly 25% of your day (and it is – it's easy math), then it is also 25% of your life. Consider that the average American will live to be 75, and subtract your age from that. For the sake of the illustration, we'll use a 35-year-old. While she may be dead tomorrow, she can anticipate another forty years of life based on averages. That means she has forty years to complete her life's goals, right? WRONG! She has 25% of forty years to complete her life's goals, remember?

Another way to number our days:

> If we have 40 years of life remaining:
> Years Available for LIVING... 10 Years!

This lady had better get busy if she has any aspirations in life. Ten years is nothing. It is a flicker. But wait! Before she can get started, we need to consider some other American pastimes. The average American family spends 3 hours and 46 minutes in front of the television each day, according to an A.C. Neilson survey in 1998. Let's say you are better than average, but we have to take this time into consideration at some level, so here goes:

Add in three hours a day for television, media, and computer use, and it leaves you with...
Less than 5 Years Remaining!

Five years of life remaining. Now, I hope that grabs you like it grabs me. If the doctor said you had five years to live, what would you do differently? We have a lot of living to do in the amount of time it takes to get from eighth-grade to high school graduation. We have some key choices to make in response to this sobering news:

1. **Get busy.** Work harder, and get as much done as possible. Well, that sounds great, but if our time is that valuable, we might want to first consider what we are busy doing.

2. **Eliminate some "life-robbers."** Now we're talking. We can add time to that five years by throwing out some of those distractions that are eating away at our years of life.

Good News: This is Not Complicated!
Let's get something straight right off the bat. Managing time effectively is simpler than you think. It is far less mysterious than many imagine. If you are looking for some elusive theory or art form that you must pursue all of your life, you are looking in the wrong place. That is not the process or goal of Home On Time. My goal for your time investment here is to look at just how basic the components of time management are, and help you learn to tackle them in a simple and realistic way that will last.

My wife and I recently organized our garage on a Saturday afternoon. It dawned on me that organizing my time does not need to be any more complicated than organizing my garage. **Just as my garage only holds a certain number of items, only a certain number of tasks will fit in my schedule.** Every page on my calendar is nothing more than a container for the tasks of my life.

Interestingly, of the three top-selling time-management books I found at my local bookstore, none included a definition of time itself. All of them began with something like this, "Time can mean many things to many people, and because of this, time management itself can mean many different things." Bologna! Is it any wonder we waste so much time if most people do not even know what it is?

Time is exactly what you think it is – it is that thing that divides one moment from the next, and keeps moments moving forward. The great physicist Albert Einstein once said that the only reason for time is so that everything doesn't happen at once. Time is going to move on whether we are managing it or not, and so it is our responsibility to use it effectively. Therefore, a workable definition of time management is equally simple to understand:

Time management is doing the right things at the right moments.

So, if time management experts around the globe have such difficulty defining time itself, how can it be so easy for Home On Time? We have the upper hand because we know the source of the information:

God Made Time
Look with me at Genesis 1, where it all started. As God was bringing the world forth out of nothing, we gain an interesting insight into time itself. What a miraculous six days it was! Day one, God created the heavens and the earth, and day and night. It would make sense that He had to create days on the very first day, or there would not have been a second day! In this light and darkness of the first day, it is worth noting that the light came from no source in particular. It simply was light because God spoke it and it was. There was no sun yet.

Not until the fourth day did God create the sun. In Genesis 1:14-18, it states, "Then God said, 'Let there be lights in the firmament of the heavens to **divide the day from the night**; and let them be for **signs and seasons**, for **days and years**; and let them be for lights in the firmament of the heavens to give light on the earth;' and it was so. Then God made two great lights: the greater light to rule the day, and the lesser light to rule the night. He made the stars also. God set them in the firmament of the heavens to give light on the earth, and to **rule over the day** and over the night, and to divide the light from the darkness. And God saw that it was good." (Emphasis Added)

Here's the point: God did not need the sun to provide light to the earth. In fact, the earth was well lit for three days without any physical light source at all. God's commanding it to be light was all that was necessary. So when the sun, moon, and stars entered the picture on day four, there was another reason altogether! **God created the sun, moon, and stars to help us divide time.** They were put there so we could manage our days, months, seasons, and even years, without a constant guessing game.

Not only did God invent time, he also invented time management. With the sun, moon, and stars, we continue to be held to God's measurements for days, months, seasons and years. He dictated a standard measure for time all the way back in creation. Have you ever noticed that there is no other standard for time – like centimeters vs. inches? There are not cultures on the other side of the world who utilize 14 hours per day because they chose a different standard. The standard is prevalent in God's creation and is unchangeable.

Here's the kicker: If time is standard, measurable, and predictable – not because we have made it so, but because God dictated that it would be so – **we can organize time just like we organize anything else that is standard, measurable, or predictable** (just like the garage!) That is BIG news!

Here's why: If we cannot really predict what time is going to do, then we can only ponder what can be done. That's how most people try to tackle their time management studies. They look for some mystical change in attitude that will suddenly bring the whole schedule into order. Instead, **we have the opportunity to oversee our management of time in measurable, attainable quantities with predictable results** – just as with some other measurable task. It was on that encouraging basis that *Home On Time: Life Management By the Book* was compiled. The items on the following pages are specific, practical tools that you can put to use right away in cleaning up your schedule.

Home On Time: Life Management By the Book was put together with one other critical assumption in mind:

You probably are not going to read this book from cover to cover.
Not to discourage you – I would be honored if you did – but very few of us ever really read the self-help books that we purchase. We just like to have them on the shelf. We carry with us the satisfaction we cared enough about ourselves to at least take the book home and look over the Table of Contents. If that is the true fate of most books, I am not going to flatter myself into assuming that you will suddenly have a strong desire to read this one from cover to cover.

Instead, this resource has been put together in order to offer the most important information first to get you started, and then to serve as a ready reference tool as you begin to customize your own schedule. The first and final sections serve as "bookends" to the entire study. These sections focus on what really matters to you: the "Balanced Life Evaluation," and the follow-up "Family Inventory." These maintenance tools help you walk through the things that matter most to you and help you point to the areas of life that need your attention.

You have permission to devour all of the life-changing information in any way you choose henceforth, but here is one recommended sequence that will allow for maximum efficiency:

1. At a minimum, read the **bold print** points and try to apply them to your own life right away. The information contained in the main text that is highlighted will be the foundation for and the springboard to all

other information contained in these sections.

2. Make up your mind right now that you are going to stick with the book until you have a realistic plan in place, and you can score higher on your Balanced Life Evaluation. If you are unwilling to honestly evaluate your life and make real changes, then you are wasting even more precious time by skimming this book. On the other hand, a little time invested with this book will offer you countless hours – perhaps years – of freedom to perform the tasks that matter to you down the road. This should be one of the easiest choices you have ever made in your life and no one can make it for you. Decide now to give this endeavor a legitimate chance to succeed.

3. Skim through each of the four sections on foundational steps to family success, and circle those aspects of life management that do not come naturally, that you need to work on, or that you are not currently doing at all. Go back to these as time dictates and see how adjustments could impact your final plan.

4. Complete the Balanced Life Evaluation BEFORE diving into this book. It will automatically point you to many of the areas on which you need to focus. This is the most important part of our time together – the opportunity to walk away with not just concepts, but a written plan for your life and a system to get that plan accomplished.

Now, fasten your seatbelt! Your life and your home will never be the same again.

Look for the "Close2Home" sections throughout this book, and you will find handy tips that are custom made for families. Looking for some practical tips that are easy to put into practice? Then "Close to Home" will be extremely valuable to you!

Close2Home

Whom Should I Trust?

There are 1.5 million more books in print today than fifty years ago, according to the RR Bowkers "Books In Print" Database. And yet while we wade through this wealth of information, are we really that much better for it? After all, if you look hard enough, you can find someone to tell you almost any advice you wish to hear.

So how can we take advantage of this wealth of wisdom that surrounds us?

- First of all, identify your greatest needs and priorities in life, and follow up with reading in that particular subject area. This may keep you from chasing opinions all over the place. For that matter, information that is inaccurate for you may be reliable for others, but for people with different goals than yours.
- Verify the source before relying on it. Many book shoppers ignore one of the important parts of any book — the "About the Author" paragraph usually found on the book jacket. Have you read mine yet? Ask yourself the question, "What gives the author the right to advise me on this subject?"
- Read online reviews. A significant number of websites now allow you to read the reviews of others who have already read the work. Of course, take this with a grain of salt, but there may be some very useful info nonetheless. By the way — that's one reason I would still stick to the printed word rather than basing my decisions on facts from the useful but often unaccountable Internet.
- And finally, if you are looking to enhance your knowledge about a particular subject, you may be able to find a fictional work that touches on the subject even as you're being entertained. For example, if you want to find out more about Civil War history, there are plenty of great novels that are accurate to the time period. Ask your librarian or bookstore consultant to point you in the right direction.

OverTime: If you are one of those people who like to dig a little deeper, then pay close attention to these sections throughout the book. We will dive in to deeper Biblical insight and study further.

The Power of a Quiet Place
I Samuel 12:16

When was the last time you sat in silence for longer than one minute, with no distractions? Today's culture undoubtedly has to go down as the most distracted generation in history. Countless voices compete for our attention night and day. Rarely do the most important ones gain the majority of it.

God commanded us to be still. To wait before we advance — to sit long enough to know the God we serve.

Put your book down, and check your watch. Spend the next five minutes focusing on the Father. Ask God to speak to you, and be still.

Look for "Time Out" sections like this one to give you extra tidbits on time. Some are just interesting information and data, and others contain quotes to ponder. You might find a reflection of your own life in these little morsels of truth!

How to Remember What You Read

"Though I do not deny that memory can be helped by places and images, yet the best memory is based on three important things: namely study, order, and care." - Erasmus wrote this in 1512. The principles will work pretty well when trying to remember the ideas in this book, too! Studies demonstrate three critical aspects to remembering information:

1. It must be studied and rehearsed. Chew on the points of the book, and mentally picture how they best apply to your own situation.

2. It must be mentally filed in some orderly fashion. Determine what areas of your life are affected by the ideas you find.

3. It must be on purpose. If you do not determine to remember something, chances are very slim that you actually will.

CHAPTER ONE

YOUR LIFE IS OUT OF CONTROL

THE POWER OF RESPONSE

Most savvy businessmen will tell you that "everything is negotiable." Unfortunately, that is not true. There are aspects of our lives that will never be in our control no matter how hard we try to negotiate them. Many people go through life with a great frustration over their inability to take hold of these things.

Death and taxes are the most popular examples, but taxes are something we actually can control. In reality, we cannot control the laws of the land. We can choose not to pay taxes, but we will be left to suffer the legal consequences. We also cannot control the stock market, other people, the boss, God, or the programming features on our VCR's.

Now, this may seem like a strange place to begin a book on time management, but it is probably the most critical aspect of all. **Until we recognize that there are aspects of life that we cannot control, we will have a very difficult time handling those things that *are* actually within our grasp.**

Isn't it interesting that if you strike up a conversation with a stranger, and you are trying to find a topic of discussion, most often one of you is going to bring up the weather? What's the big deal about the weather that we go on and on about it? We are so fascinated that there is actually a 24-hour TV channel where we can learn not only about our own weather, but weather patterns on the other side of the country! Why is that? I believe our fascination with the weather lies in the fact that we cannot control it, but it affects our lives. **We are obsessed with our lack of control.**

Close2Home

In the business of family life, we often forget to plan for the forces we will encounter each day. Without closely managing our activities, we will pay dearly. Make sure you leave room on your daily schedule to manage that schedule. Along the same lines, over-filling your schedule leaves you no time to respond to those surprises you did not anticipate. Plan enough downtime so you are able to respond with wisdom.

On the other hand, many things that are completely within our control escape our attention every day. We have total control over what food goes in our mouths during a given day. We also have full knowledge that the food we take in will have great bearing on our health and longevity. Yet many, if not most, Americans ingest "supersized" menus as if we have no clue that they greatly increase risk of obesity and heart disease. We seem to be unaware of our ability to control many important areas of our lives. Maybe it is because we are too busy talking about the weather!

I am reminded of the seventh chapter of the book of Romans, in which Paul talks about how frustrating it is when we do things we really do not want to do. We may know we do not need to eat another unhealthy dessert, but we find ourselves doing it anyway. We know we need to get up in the morning, but we hit the "snooze" button seven times.

The Word of God is clear: We are called to be people who control ourselves. The word self-control simply means we do not need others to restrain us because we are able to show our own restraint. If we mess up, it is no one's fault but our own. When it comes to inaction, it often simply comes down to good old lack of discipline on our part.

If there is one aspect of the Home On Time concept that separates it from all other time management tools on the

> "I must govern the clock, not be governed by it."
> Golda Meir

market today, it is this important aspect: **As Christians, God never promised us that we could take complete control of our lives.** In fact, when we came to Christ, we gave up all control in exchange for the freeing control of our Savior – the Lord Jesus Christ. Instead of trying to be in control, we must seek to respond to God's control. That means adjusting our plans to accommodate His plans, building our calendars around His priorities, and walking away from things that do not matter.

This is the essence of "The Power of Response" – the first critical pillar of time management. **In order to respond effectively to the world around us, we have to recognize the difference between what we can control and what we cannot control.** Then we have to learn to adapt our plans to those things out of our control, and take hold of those things God has placed under our control.

If you have ever read anything on the management of time, chances are good that you have not seen anything related to response in the program guide. Most resources are trying to teach you to control every aspect of your life. Unfortunately, that is an impossible goal. You can never be content with life if you do not get this point first, because you will always be frustrated. Write this on your heart and never forget it:

Most of life is out of control.

You cannot dictate success in areas where you have no control. You will never be able to make it a goal of yours to stay healthy, stay wealthy, be popular with everyone, raise perfect

POWER OF RESPONSE   31

Get your attention off those things that are none of your business.

"Anything that is wasted effort represents wasted time." – Ted Engstrom, author of *The Pursuit of Excellence*

Make sure that everything you allow to influence your life will help you reach your long-term goals. If a force conflicts with your goals, it is not worthy of your time.

children, or escape heartache. All of those dreams – and any others you can think of – will involve factors that you could not possibly manipulate.

In fact, as Christians, we are never meant to be in complete control of our surroundings. We are instead called to respond appropriately to what happens around us. We are told in I Peter 3:15 that we should "always be ready to give a defense to everyone who asks you a reason for the hope that is in you, with meekness and fear." **In other words, our ability to be prepared with answers for life will determine success or failure in our Christian walk.** During this section, we will learn both when and how to respond.

Before we dive in, however, we must recognize that some issues that are completely out of our control are not even worth a response. This simple truth might possibly save you more time than any other principle in the entire text.

Most of life is none of your business.

That is right – for most of the issues that are out of our

control, we need to just get over it. The rude lady that irritates you at church is not your problem. She has no control over you unless you allow her to, and you are not going to change her anyway!

I played basketball in high school, and I suppose like most kids I thought I was pretty good. Toward the beginning of my junior season, we headed to New Braunfels, Texas to play in a tournament – one that we had every intention of winning with relative ease. At six-foot-five, I played in the center position, and so I always identified the tallest guy

Psalm 90 is the oldest Psalm in the entire book. Moses was probably toward the end of his 120 years when he penned this incredible work. The ninetieth Psalm, in my opinion, is the greatest insight into productive time management ever written down. And who better to write down the Word of God on this topic than Moses? Here was a man who had seen it all – adopted to escape infanticide, but trained in Judaism by his mother/babysitter, raised by royalty, exiled by a reactionary murder, married in Midian, a shepherd in the desert, called by God on Mt. Sinai, the deliverer of the Jews, their leader back in the desert – a place he knew well – and God's spokesman for His covenant with His people. He had seen the best and worst of people, he had seen people break commitments, he had seen God's grace give them second chances, and he had seen God work indescribable wonders among the people. Moses' life gave him multiple perspectives from which to share this incredible insight into the challenge of time management.

on the other team's roster right away as the one I would be guarding most of my time in the game. Well, our first game was against a tiny San Antonio high school whose big man was a six-foot-nine guy named Shaquille O'Neal. I had never heard of him at this point in his career, but I have never forgotten him either. He blocked my shot harder than it had ever been blocked and more times than I care to remember. He scored at will. I had absolutely no control over what he did during that humiliating game. Looking back now, I can also see what he has done to the very best players on the planet over the past decade, and it certainly puts it in perspective.

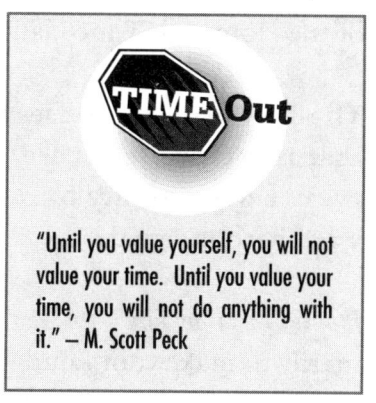

"Until you value yourself, you will not value your time. Until you value your time, you will not do anything with it." – M. Scott Peck

Still, the memory of competing with one of the greatest players in history has helped me realize an important truth about life:

There are some areas of life that are out of your control but affect your life in a big way.

These forces cannot be ignored. Just as I was unable to control Shaq and had no response to his combination of strength, size, and quickness, I have areas of my life that seem to dominate what I do and how I spend my time. Shaq was basically unbeatable, and some of the forces in

"Hard work is often the the easy work you did not do at the proper time."
Bernard Meltzer

your life are unbeatable too. You will have to simply learn to play around them. Even today, teams who beat Shaquille O'Neal usually respond by playing around him, moving the offense away from him, and trying to keep the ball out of his hands – making him less of a factor in the game. The thought of uncontrollable forces in life brings a feeling of dread, and the preoccupation we feel toward these issues often negatively affects our other essential tasks. The secret of effective time management is to identify these giants in the game of life and respond appropriately. That is the core of our goal in the Response section of the Home On Time Plan:

The Power of Response: By identifying those things that affect my life but are out of my control, I will have greater opportunity to respond wisely as I move forward with my goals.

Home On Time: Life Management By the Book is designed primarily to make your family life more productive and successful, but there is no way to do that without addressing every aspect of life management – home, work, church, hobbies, friends, and every other place you live. Fortunately, we have a trustworthy text that encompasses all of those things.

> "Time is one thing that can never be retrieved. One may lose and regain friends. One may lose and regain money. Opportunity, once spurned, may come again. But the hours that are lost in idleness can never be brought back to be used in gainful pursuits."
>
> Winston Churchill

As we dive into Psalm 90, Moses begins with a very depressing picture – he demonstrates the perspective of mankind in his losing battle with time. He identifies some key areas in which our lack of control is manifested. As we walk through the passage, we will want to take note of the key pictures listed. The pictures are easy to spot, because they all start with the word "like." He is comparing time and life to specific symbols that we will need to identify.

How often does time go fast when you want it to go slow and go slow when you want it to go fast?

Remember when you were a kid, and grown-ups would not let you swim for an hour after eating? What was that all about, anyway?

After all, did you ever hear of some kid drowning because he had just eaten? "Poor Tommy. He took a bite of that sandwich and then jumped in the water. Went right to the bottom like a brick. Should have waited the standard sixty minutes, and he'd be standing here today." Did our parents think we were that bad at swimming, that the extra 10 ounces of bologna in our stomachs was going to put us over the edge? If that's the case, a kid shouldn't be in the water anyway. Ironically, you could get out and drink some water with no time penalty at all. Seems like water would weigh more than food – and that's what sinks ships. In all the movies, the ship fills up with water just before it goes to the bottom. You never hear the captain shouting "get rid of the lunch meat! Throw it overboard! We're all going to sink!" Nope – it's the water that does the trick. I'm going to make my kids stay out of the water, if anything at all.

Verses one through six read as follows in the New King James Version:

> "¹ A Prayer of Moses the man of God. Lord, You have been our dwelling place in all generations.
>
> ²Before the mountains were brought forth, Or ever You had formed the earth and the world, Even from everlasting to everlasting, You are God.

Right away, we establish something rather obvious. God was here first. I cannot expect to control Him. To believe otherwise would be very naive. While we have been given the awesome privilege of prayer, in which we have the opportunity to ask for His hand in our lives, our principle role with God is to respond to Him – and not vice-versa.

> ³ You turn man to destruction, and say, "Return, O children of men." ⁴ For a thousand years in Your sight are like yesterday when it is past, And like a watch in the night.
>
> ⁵ You carry them away like a flood; They are like a sleep.
>
> In the morning they are like grass which grows up: ⁶ In the morning it flourishes and grows up; In the evening it is cut down and withers."

What a dreadful picture of life, and yet that is how many view it. This picture illustrates the way most people I know live their lives – what I call "A Pitiful Picture of a Pinball Person." When you are playing pinball, you really

Pinball Picture	Reactionary Result
"Watch in the Night"	Unaware
"Flood"	Surprised
"Sleep"	Helpless
"Grass"	Fragile

have very little control over what happens to that small metal ball. Once you pull back the hammer and let it go, the ball is left to the whims and chance of where it bounces and ricochets. People find themselves in a lifestyle of bouncing from the most urgent need to the next just like that pinball – clinging to the hope that their performance will be satisfactory before the game ends. This constant battle with time, Moses contends, is really an ongoing battle with God Himself – and God always wins. Plodding through life with the dreadful notion that God, and the time He created, has become our adversary is no way to live.

Now, we have circled some very distinct characteristics of dread-filled living that Moses mentions in this painful introduction. Here are some of the key pictures as they relate to how we view time:

A WATCH IN THE NIGHT

This first picture is an interesting one. If you read about this passage in many Bible commentaries, they will indicate that a watch in the night is four hours. The idea here, then, would be that compared to a thousand years, or even a day, a watch in the night is a short period of time.

> "And in the end, it's not the years in your life that count. It's the life in your years."
>
> Abraham Lincoln

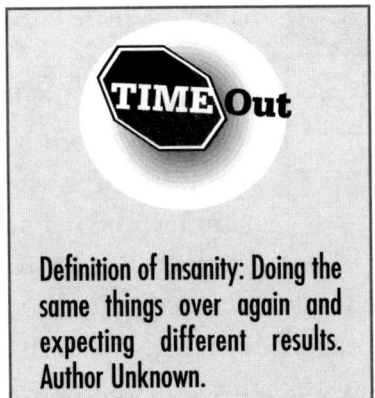

Definition of Insanity: Doing the same things over again and expecting different results. Author Unknown.

Still, I do not think that tells the whole story.

Imagine standing guard over an ancient village in the middle of the night for four hours. That is a watch in the night. Now, the first night may be pretty exciting, but after that, I doubt there is much action. I can imagine a lot of battles with boredom as the night drags on. Now hear me – I do not think that Moses means that time goes slowly – although it could mean that.

I think Moses was going further than just describing the length of a watch in the night. The two closest references to a watch in the night are found in Exodus 14 and Judges 9. In Exodus 14, the Egyptian Army was in the middle of crossing the Red Sea when God removed their chariot wheels during the night watch. There was more a sense of confusion than any length of time. They simply could not see! The reference in Judges 9 is to Gideon's very small army surrounding a city during a watch in the night. If you remember the story, when the army blew their trumpets, the Midianites were so confused and frightened that they ran out of the city, and Gideon's army easily slaugh-

> "There are a million ways to lose a work day, but not even a single way to get one back."
>
> Tom DeMarco & Timothy Lister

tered them. The army of Midian could no doubt have conquered Gideon's, but because they were unaware of the facts they were defeated.

I believe that is the connotation of the "watch in the night" in Psalm 90. I think that time often becomes the enemy because we are unaware – because we cannot see it. Moses is trying to make the point of the speed at which time can fly by, and he gives us this important insight. **When we are paying close attention, time seems to slow down. But when we are not paying attention, time goes by much faster.** Remember the old saying, "A watched pot never boils?" Well, Moses is contending that the opposite is true: An ignored pot boils over before you know it.

When we think of "watch in the night," unaware would be an accurate one-word description. The sad first truth of pinball living is that oftentimes we do not have a clue what is happening and which forces are pushing us through life.

THE FLOOD PICTURE

In a flood, life can unexpectedly take a turn for the worse. In July of 2002, my family moved back to Texas.

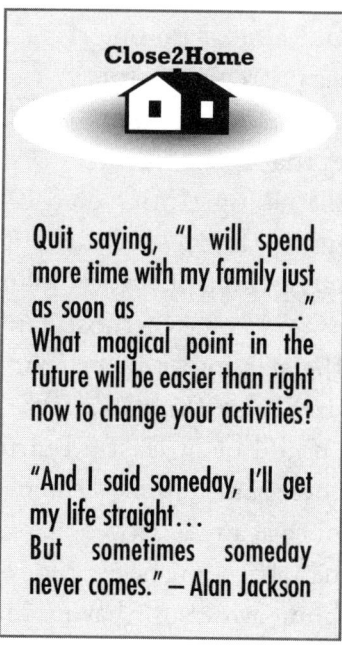

Close2Home

Quit saying, "I will spend more time with my family just as soon as _____."
What magical point in the future will be easier than right now to change your activities?

"And I said someday, I'll get my life straight...
But sometimes someday never comes." – Alan Jackson

We were settling in to being back home again. It had not rained more than an inch in the three months since we arrived, and the entire state was steeped in a record drought. I traveled back to Virginia one Saturday afternoon to record some radio and television programs. On my way to the airport, it began to rain. During my four days away from home, the area where we live in Central Texas received over 30 inches of rain! Needless to say, just about every creek and river in the area overflowed, many lost their homes, and the governor estimated over one billion dollars in damage. Even for those of us who did not experience the damage firsthand, many roadways were shut down – rendering most of the state unable to travel anywhere. This seemed almost impossible considering the extreme dry conditions we had been experiencing, and almost no one was prepared for the onslaught. Perhaps the most

Pinball Picture	Reactionary Result
"Watch in the Night"	Unaware
"Flood"	Surprised
"Sleep"	Helpless
"Grass"	Fragile

intriguing stories of the flood began about four years prior. In 1998, Central Texas had experienced another large flood in which many riverside houses were swept away. Some of those same homeowners had rebuilt on the existing site – believing the storm to be of the "hundred year flood" variety – meaning that another flood should be at least a century away. Just four years later, these same families watched in horror as their homes were once again destroyed, like a surreal "instant replay" button had been pushed. Many in the media criticized those homeowners for having made the same mistake twice, yet some of the homeowners were already planning to rebuild in the same area again. **In much the same way, we are all guilty of areas in life where we continue making the same errors over and over again, with little anticipation and continued surprise at the results!**

A flood is an unexpected phenomena, and that is why it can be so deadly. In the same way, our lives can take very unpredictable twists and turns – and often we are ill-prepared for what is coming. Moses paints this second picture of how we respond to life to show us an interesting parallel. Like the flash flood that shut down Central Texas, a lack of anticipation carries away much of our lives – rendering us incapable of reaching our goals.

There are, of course, some things that we can never really be ready for. The attack of September 11, 2001, was one of those events that no one saw coming. While it had an enormous impact on the psyche of every American, it was hardly something that could have been prepared for. At the same time, while there are many things in life that should be fairly easy to anticipate, many among us seem to be equally flabbergasted when they happen. When you send your child onto the carpet with a glass of red Kool-Aid, there really should not be extreme shock when the permanent stain ends up on the floor. Most former students have memories of staying up all night to finish projects or study for exams that had been scheduled weeks – even months – in advance. Most of us will one day be unable to work, but many Americans are ill-prepared financially for retirement.

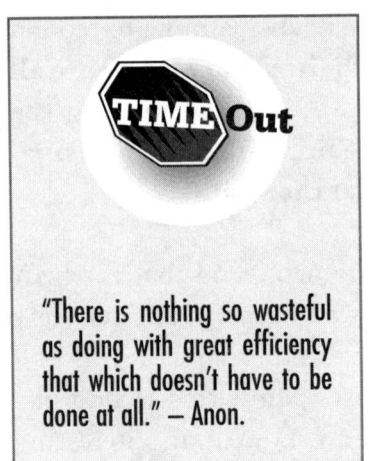

"There is nothing so wasteful as doing with great efficiency that which doesn't have to be done at all." – Anon.

The flood picture in our "Pinball Chart" needs the word surprise. A lack of anticipation often leads to disaster far more devastating than is necessary.

THE SLEEP PICTURE

In 1997 Scott Falater of Arizona was accused of brutally stabbing and then drowning his wife in the middle of the night. When the case came to trial, Scott never denied the killing, but did plead not guilty. Instead, Scott claimed that he had been sleepwalking, and that his actions were completely out of his control. The jury found 44-year-old Scott Falater guilty of first degree murder in 1999 - regardless of the excuse.

(From ABC News, transcript found on abcnews.com, Copyright ©1999 ABC News Internet Ventures, New York, NY)

Sleep is illustrative of a time when we are out of control. It is also a period of life when time seems to pass us by. Moses is asserting that this lack of control ends up robbing us of much of our lives. While hopefully the results are far less devastating than those of Mr. Falater's actions, we can be assured that our lives – even if they feel helpless and out of control – are still our own responsibility. We will

> "Half our life is spent trying to find something to do with the time we have rushed through life trying to save."
> Will Rogers

be held accountable for our actions or inactions regardless of how helpless we may feel.

Pinball Picture	Reactionary Result
"Watch in the Night"	Unaware
"Flood"	Surprised
"Sleep"	Helpless
"Grass"	Fragile

Moses is saying that often life is wasted because we treat time as if we have no control over where it goes. We are in a constant state of reaction to the forces at work around us – with little or no influence on where those forces take us. And as a result, we find ourselves in a culture that blames everything that happens on someone else. If you are a drug addict, it is because of the stress. If you are a sex addict, it is because you were abused as a child. We have an excuse in place for every major vice in our culture today – primarily because we have bought into this same trap that Moses talks about in the 90th Psalm. We are a generation of reactors.

The sleep picture is characterized by a feeling of helplessness. Helplessness is a major part of pinball living.

There is one more picture in this first series of verses that I want to look at.

THE GRASS PICTURE

The end of verse 5 continuing into verse 6 Moses says, "In the morning they are like grass which grows up; in the evening it is cut down and withers."

When conditions are not exactly right, grass is a very delicate plant. It is easily disturbed and famously fickle. As

Matthew Henry said in his famous commentary of this passage, "That it is a short and transient life, like that of the grass which grows up and flourishes, in the morning looks green and pleasant, but in the evening the mower cuts it down, and it immediately withers, changes its colour, and loses all its beauty. Death will change us shortly, perhaps suddenly; and it is a great change that death will make with us in a little time. Man, in his prime, does but flourish as the grass, which is weak, and low, and tender, and exposed, and which, when the winter of old age comes, will wither of itself: but he may be mown down by disease or disaster, as the grass is, in the midst of summer. All flesh is as grass."

Like the grass picture in verses five and six, our life can be delicate and fragile when we find our reflection in the "Pitiful Picture of Pinball Living." Next on our chart, we will mark the grass picture with the word fragile.

Now that the Pinball Living chart is complete, you should have the full pitiful picture in front of you: The words unaware, surprised, helpless, and fragile describe a life you do not want – one that is totally controlled by outside forces.

A NEW CHOICE!

So what is our alternative? **We can, instead of reacting, choose to respond.**

To illustrate the difference between the two, let's rewind for a moment in the author's life. We can look at a picture of both examples at different stages of his lifetime. At the age of forty, after Moses had been raised by the Pharaoh's

There are two key areas of life that can have a tremendous impact on our anticipation:

Milestones. Every parent can anticipate some specific events in a child's life that will be very significant. Starting school, moving into Junior High, and getting a driver's license are some examples most can relate to. They are special times in our culture in which a significant change in status takes place. If parents can attach important spiritual events to these important times, then they can gain a great advantage. Joe White, President of Kanakuk Camps, offered to buy his children a car on their sixteenth birthday if they would memorize two books of the Bible.

Seasons. Closely related to milestones, seasons are time periods in our calendars that provide prime opportunities for certain goals to be accomplished. In the life of a farmer, crops cannot be planted and harvested on a whim. They have specific times in which success is a greater possibility. Without identifying these key seasons, farmers can never be successful. In the same way, we must identify the points of time in which we have the greatest chance for success. This can happen in the context of a calendar year — family vacations usually have to happen when school is not in session, for example. They can also be identified in a broader sense, along the entire life span. Women can only fulfill a desire to bear children for a certain window of the life span, for example. Missing this opportunity greatly reduces the chance of parenting. I have found many older men in my work as a pastor who are looking to make a significant contribution during the "fourth quarter" of life. They are uniquely qualified to fill some essential roles in their churches and communities, given the opportunity. By anticipating seasons of life, we can increase our chances of reaching our goals by targeting windows of opportunity.

daughter, having had access to all the riches and plenty that went with it, Moses began to realize the plight and difficulties of his fellow Jews – who were being used to do the work of pack animals in the name of Pharaoh's building projects. Moses saw a wrong in the society around him. Now that was noble, but his reaction was not good. Without much thought for the options he might have had to bring about change, Moses simply reacted in an emotional stupor. He killed an Egyptian and ended up having to flee to Midian – all of his influence for change having been thrown away. Moses reacted with little thought or prayer.

Fast-forward some forty years later – Moses has been placed by God at the helm of the Israelites as they are fleeing Egypt and its evil leader. As we peer into Exodus chapter 14, they have found themselves at the banks of the Red Sea, with no hope for escape from Pharaoh's pursuing army except the Divine intervention of Almighty God. By this time in Moses' life, he has the wisdom to respond to the situation at hand in a way that brings victory and a long-term positive result.

We need to notice something important at this point. In both instances of Moses' life, the passions he acted on were born out of the same convictions. **The angry reaction ended in failure, while the wise response ended in a success that Jews still celebrate today.** The difference seems to lie in how Moses responded.

In the same way, many people I come across today are concerned about the same things. They want their marriages

> "You can't do anything about the length of your life, but you can do something about it's width and depth."
> Shira Tehrani

to last. They honestly want their children to turn out okay. They want to see their communities improved and to see injustices around them corrected. And yet a large portion of the families I come across today are completely frustrated with their inability to act on those wholesome desires. They feel ill-equipped or even hopeless in managing their time and lives effectively.

Close2Home

Some friends of ours have found a way to beat the rush that goes with having active kids in the home. They meet from time to time and have breakfast, taking the opportunity to share what God is doing in each of their lives. "Everyone is eating breakfast anyway," says the dad, "so we decided that with just a little more effort, we could make that a time to share as a family." In doing so, they have discovered something small that may pay huge dividends while responding to the challenges of a crowded calendar. Look around at the mundane things in your everyday life, and search for simple ways to expand your family time!

We should realize by now that much of what happens in our lives will be out of our control. It comes down to how we respond to a given situation. To illustrate the point further, let's look at what Webster's Dictionary says about the two closely related terms:

To react is to *offer resistance or opposition to a force*.
To respond is literally to *give an answer*.

(From Merriam Webster Online (www.Merriam-Webster.com) copyright 2002 by Merriam-Webster, Incorporated, Taken from Collegiate Dictionary copyright © 2001 by Merriam-Webster, Incorporated, Springfield, MA)

Reactions can be performed by any number of inanimate objects, because there is no control involved. Any reaction is directly proportional to the acting force – literally a RE-Action. A response takes maturity and intelligence. It does not have to correspond to the acting force at all. As you will see through the truths in God's word, the line between success and failure is often the difference between a reaction and a response.

The difference between responding and reacting can best be described with the following:

	Reacting	VS	Responding
Motive	Fear		Calling
Attitude	Dread		Expectation
Action	Chaotic		Controlled
Source	Circumstances		Wisdom
1st Step	Guesswork		Purposeful

All of this contrast between reacting and responding leaves us with a very important rule about time management.

Rather than going through life as if we are out of control – largely incapable of controlling our responses to all of the forces around us – we now have a positive option:

God has given us the ability to respond with wisdom to forces affecting our lives. We have the freedom to choose a course of action that is completely independent of what others are doing.

Pinball Picture	Reactionary Result	Response Opportunity
"Watch in the Night"	Unaware	Awareness
"Flood"	Surprised	Anticipation
"Sleep"	Helpless	Adaptation
"Grass"	Fragile	Tenacity

Just as the ability to respond greatly affected Moses' measure of success, our newfound insight into responding can show us the way to a different lifestyle than "pinball living"!

Look back up at the pinball living chart we filled in earlier. Next to the "Pinball Chart" column, we need to add a "Response Opportunity" column that offers the positive alternative. Sometimes in the Bible, God tells us exactly what to do. Other times, He gives us a clear picture of how NOT to live. I believe this is one of those pictures in Scripture that God wants us to take and turn inside-out – discovering a positive contradiction to a negative picture.

UNAWARENESS TO AWARENESS

Moses gave us a picture of a watch in the night – a picture showing someone who is unaware. On the contrary, our goal for overcoming this danger would be just the opposite. **By seeking to maintain an awareness of the forces around us, we will have an opportunity to prepare a response.**

> "When you have to make a choice and don't make it, that is in itself a choice."
> William James

SURPRISE TO ANTICIPATION

Next, Moses gave us a picture of a flood, in which he illustrates that people are often surprised. In a positive light, the opposite of this assertion would be a desire to anticipate what is coming, allowing us to be prepared for maximum effectiveness in an upcoming situation. **Our ability to anticipate what is coming will greatly increase our effectiveness with the time we are allotted.** So anticipation is our next key word on the chart.

> **Close2Home**
>
> Difficult decisions are a way of life in the world of parenting. Remember – sometimes making a wrong decision is better than making no decision at all. The world is full of regretful parents who avoided the "tough issues" that ended in painful consequences.
>
> "Sometimes you have to make the right decision, and sometimes you have to make the decision right." – Dr. Phil McGraw

HELPLESSNESS TO ADAPTATION

Now for the sleep picture. What is the opposite of helplessness? Well, you may be tempted to say control, but that is not always possible. Remember – we have to learn to respond to those things we cannot control! In real life, the opposite of helplessness is adaptation, and that is where we will focus. **We need to learn to adapt to the forces around us if we are going to be productive and successful.** Adaptation is our key word under the response column.

> Forewarned, forearmed; to be prepared is half the victory.
> **Cervantes**

Pinball Picture	Reactionary Result	Response Opportunity
"Watch in the Night"	Unaware	Awareness
"Flood"	Surprised	Anticipation
"Sleep"	Helpless	Adaptation
"Grass"	Fragile	Tenacity

A few years ago, while working on the family budget, I was frustrated at how much we were spending on gasoline every month. It seemed like such a fruitless expense to me: who gets excited about the gas they've consumed. At first I was angry with the gas companies for such high costs per gallon, but this fact was obviously completely out of my control. What I could control, however, was the amount of gas I consumed. I decided to sell my beloved Dodge Ram 4X4 because the fuel economy was horrible, and get a more fuel-efficient ride. By adapting my vehicle, I saved nearly one hundred dollars out of the monthly gas budget!

FRAGILITY TO TENACITY

Our final picture was grass – a picture illustrating how fragile our lives can be. Of course, the contrast here is something that any successful responder has to discover: tenacity. Tenacity is a great word, because it describes a tough-mindedness that is not easily shaken. Tenacious people move forward despite obstacles, and that is what we need.

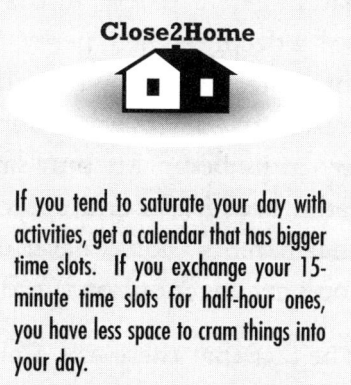

Close2Home

If you tend to saturate your day with activities, get a calendar that has bigger time slots. If you exchange your 15-minute time slots for half-hour ones, you have less space to cram things into your day.

Remember the story about my gas-guzzling pick-up truck? There was a little bit more to that story. As much as I loved that truck, I knew it had to go. Lana and I looked at several cars, and settled on a good-looking Dodge Intrepid. We made the trade at the Dodge dealership, and pulled off the lot with the whole family in our new vehicle. On the way home, I asked Lana if she minded if we stopped by the church to pick up my guitar – mainly as an excuse to drive the new vehicle just a little longer before parking it for the day.

We ran into my office and came right back out. Everybody sort of went their own direction – Lana to her door, Ryley to hers, and I went to the trunk to insert the guitar. Reagan, our then five-year-old, held back at the front of the car, and when I got done with the trunk I called her inside. She walked slowly over, and had something in her hand. When she got in, Lana just sensed that something was up and asked what she was carrying. Reagan handed over a small, jagged rock without making eye contact. Lana instinctively told me to stop the car. She bounded out and inspected the area where Reagan had lingered. There on the center of our new car's hood was a deeply etched, perfectly formed four-inch "R" – left for posterity. To say I was upset would be a gross understatement. There was a burning sensation that overtook my entire body. My only saving thoughts were the many radio broadcasts and speeches in which I had declared that parents should never discipline in anger. Instead, I took my anger out on our driving speed as I raced home.

The fact that there was a mark on my car was out of my control at that point. How I responded to my daughter was completely in my control, however. It was at that point that I had to choose between reacting and responding. Before I did anything that would have scarred my daughter for life, we had a long talk and an appropriate disciplinary action was handed out – no pun intended!

When it was all said and done, Reagan felt great remorse, and a long discussion about the prison time served by most repeat vandals seemed to drive home the message. Had a stranger so defamed my new car, I can say with nearly absolute confidence that my anger would have manifested itself much more overtly – probably to a fault. My love for Reagan was infinitely greater than her offense toward me, and understanding my priorities helped me proceed appropriately. In fact, my large R became such a conversation piece I didn't even buff it out completely.

I am thankful that our Heavenly Father, while not keeping us out of trouble, will walk with us through the messes we've created ourselves. The grace of the Father has no real comparison. He has a tenacious love for you that cannot be shaken, and it is indicated in how He responds to us, His children.

Your ability to respond will ultimately determine your ability to move forward with the planning process. No matter how organized your calendar becomes, your lack of power in predicting the future will dash holes in your plans if you are not ready to respond.

If the idea of a personal relationship with God is new to you, please take the time to read chapter five, "The Greatest News in the Entire Book."

CHAPTER TWO

HOW DO I GET THERE FROM HERE?

THE POWER OF DIRECTION

As a teenager in Lockhart, Texas, my greatest weekend pastime was "cruising." Most small-town alumni probably have similar memories, because there just was not much to do on the weekends. To fill up the time, we would just drive up and down Highway 183, with regular detours through the Town Square, for hours at a time.

The goals of cruising were simple:

- My friends and I were looking for girls who might also be cruising. The hunt for girls was a critical element. The thought of simply calling them on the phone and making contact to avoid this hunt never crossed our minds.

- To demonstrate to other teenagers that we had access to a car. This seemed, for some reason, like a very proud statement at the age of sixteen.

- To demonstrate that we could turn up our radios to the point where all the citizens of Lockhart could enjoy our musical selections for the evening.

Keep Your Eyes on the Big Picture

You need to ask yourself whether each small goal you set is really helping you reach a long-term goal.

That was about it. Looking back now, it is amazing to me that we would spend that much time driving in a car and really go nowhere. It takes about four hours to drive to Dallas from my childhood home, but I drove six blocks in about the same amount of time!

Cruising is a forgivable waste of time while in high school, but cruising through life has much more regrettable consequences. This essential truth is the springboard into the next Home On Time principle:

By clarifying the most important things in my life, and the direction that I want to take in the days ahead, I can make sound decisions about what actions should be taken and what burdens should be left behind.

"The Wandering Picture"

When we left off in Psalm 90, Moses had painted a sad

picture of what I called "pinball living" – this idea of life flying by and ending before we are ready. The next section begins to reveal the context of this pitiful picture. After God delivered the Hebrew children out of slavery in Egypt, brought them across the Red Sea, and delivered them to the very door of the Promised Land about a year later, the Jews failed to believe that God could deliver them the rest of the way. After sending twelve spies into the land, the Israelites decided it would be too dangerous to move forward in obedience. As a result, the Jews were sentenced to forty years of wilderness wandering. And furthermore, no one over the age of twenty at the beginning of this wandering would be allowed to enter the Promised Land, with the exception of Joshua and Caleb.

Most scholars believe this Psalm was written some time after a major failure at Kadesh-barnea (Numbers 13-14), and that sheds new light on the next verses:

> "For we have been consumed by Your anger, And by Your wrath we are terrified. You have set our iniquities before You, our secret sins in the light of Your countenance. For all our days have passed away in Your wrath; we finish our years like a sigh. The days of our lives are seventy years; and if by reason of strength they are eighty years, yet their boast is only labor and sorrow; for it is soon cut off, and we fly away. Who knows the power of Your anger? For as the fear of You, so is Your wrath."

If Moses wrote this toward the end of his life, then he was well beyond one hundred years old. So the reference to living seventy or eighty years would not be logical without our new insight, because all the adults were basically given a death sentence sometime during the forty-year journey. They had absolutely no chance of reaching their goals. The Israelites were wanderers in every sense of the word.

Fast forward to the cross. **When we read these words in light of what Christ has done for us, we no longer have to live under the hopelessness of condemnation. We do not *have* to wander!** God has given us everything we need for life and godliness. We have a golden opportunity every day to pursue the will of God for our lives.

Paul put it this way: "Not that I have already attained, or am already perfected; but I press on, that I may lay hold of that for which Christ Jesus has also laid hold of me." (Phil. 3:12) He is speaking not of a wandering, but a glorious, goal-oriented striving toward godliness!

The difference between wandering and striving is simply the presence of a goal. That pretty much illustrates my feeling about exercise. I despise jogging, because there is generally no competition, motivation, or winners circle. It requires tremendous effort for me, even when it is my only alternative for cardiovascular exercise. On the other hand, I love to play basketball. Even at this point in my life when I am not up for any all-star status, it is a great pleasure of mine to move up and down the floor. Honestly, I probably expend twice the energy in basketball as I do in jogging, but I do it with energy and exuberance because I have a goal in mind. In the short term, there are baskets to shoot and defense to play. In the long term, I want to win the game.

Jesus said it best when He called us to follow Him in Matthew 11:28-30:

> "Come to me, all you who labor and are heavy laden, and I will give you rest. Take my yoke upon you and learn from Me, for I am gentle and lowly in heart, and you will find rest for your souls. For my yoke is easy and my burden is light."

Jesus is not speaking of the yoke that comes with labor, but the freedom and privilege of working toward an eternal goal. This made the request not one to be dreaded, but highly anticipated. This incredible contrast can be summed up in one important truth:

Your sense of purpose determines the difference between hopeless labor and focused living.

What is God's will and purpose for you? For your family? What are the most important things in your life? How do you want to be remembered by future generations? If you could pass on just five principles to your children, what would they be?

> "Much has been given us, and much will rightfully be expected from us. We have duties to others and duties to ourselves; and we can shirk neither."
> Theodore Roosevelt

Do You Know What You Really Want?

Taking a long hard look at what you desire out of life will help give substance to the goals you set.

"The first step to getting the things you want out of life is this – decide what you want." – Ben Stein

Answers to these simple questions are essential to the formation of a successful family calendar. This may be the most critical step in the process of moving toward success. After all, if you are moving in the right DIRECTION, even if you are moving very slowly, at least you will be closer than you were before! If you get the other steps right, but are moving in the wrong direction, all your efforts will be wasted.

In order to determine the direction we will map out in the following section, we need to establish two essentials on which to build:

>Our Roles – The responsibilities and relationships that are most essential in our lives.

>Our Goals – The outcomes of my life that will allow us to fulfill our purpose for being here.

"Role Call"

In a given day, I fill many different roles. I am husband,

"It is not length of life, but depth of life."
   Ralph Waldo Emerson

father, son, writer, consultant, minister, consumer, and much more. Try to list all the roles you may assume in a given day:

_____

_____

_____

_____

These roles determine the majority of your actions throughout the day. **How you prioritize these roles will ultimately determine your accomplishments in life!**

After high school, I attended a small university primarily because I had the opportunity to play basketball on scholarship. I felt I could step right in and play a key role on the team. I arrived to a different story. The players were much better than I had anticipated (and perhaps I was not as good as I had suspected!), and I spent much of the season sitting on the bench, a helpless observer.

About halfway through my freshmen season, I got up the nerve to ask my coach for more playing time – convinced I could make an impact on the team. After practice one day, I approached Coach Leach (yes – that was really his name!) and asked for a word. I then began a well-rehearsed pitch: "Coach, I truly believe I can make this

---

"Anything that is wasted effort represents wasted time. The best management of our time thus becomes linked inseparably with the best utilization of our efforts."

Ted W. Engstrom

team better. What steps can I take to make a greater contribution in games?" Even looking back now, I admire the smoothness of my bold request! Unfortunately, Coach Leach's response was equally smooth.

> "Ryan, what is my job on this team?"
> "To make us winners, Coach."
> "That's right, Ryan. I want to make you a winner in life, but my job really depends on us winning on the basketball court. (I was getting nervous. He was still smiling, but I saw punishment in the future for my boldness.) Ryan, how many players are on this team?
> "Eighteen, sir."
> "That's right. And how many can play at once?" (Now he was asking me stupid questions, and I felt less like a smooth orator and more like a kindergartner!)
> "Five, sir."
> "Right again! So if my goal is to win the game, and I can only play five at a time, which ones do you think I'm going to play?"
> "The best players."
> "Exactly. I've got to play the players that I believe are going to give me the greatest chance at a victory. Understand?"

When I walked away from the coach, it dawned on me what he had just explained. I was on the bench because I was not good enough to play. And on the bench is where I stayed most of my freshman season!

While I still believe I could have helped my team that year, Coach Leach presented a great illustration about life. **We**

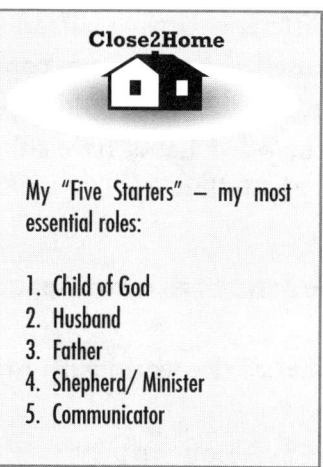

My "Five Starters" – my most essential roles:

1. Child of God
2. Husband
3. Father
4. Shepherd/ Minister
5. Communicator

all have a limited amount of time in which to win or lose, and we all have to determine who our starters are going to be. In life, those starters are the essential roles that need to command most of your "game time." These are the roles that give you the greatest opportunity for victory in life. On the other hand, some of the roles you listed earlier do not deserve much playing time at all. They are unessential at best and detrimental to your goals at worst.

Look back at the list of roles you made earlier. Prayerfully consider roles that are most essential to your lifetime success. In other words, when you die, which five roles will you wish you had invested in most significantly? Yes, you MUST limit it to five roles. No, you may not combine your spouse and parent roles - they are two distinct and special callings.

List your own "Five Starters:
_____
_____
_____
_____
_____

"Goal Call"

We all have dreams – things we would love to see happen in

our lives. There is a tremendous difference between dreams and goals, and they are often confused. A dream is not concrete or defined. It is simply something we wish would happen down the road. Goals, on the other hand, have substance. They are characterized by the following:

1. **Goals are defined by the actions that will make them a reality.**
   a. Dream: – "I want to see the world with my family."
   b. Goal: – "I want to make one trip every six months for the next ten years with my family in order to see the world."

2. **Goals are measurable.**
   a. Dream: "I want to lose weight this year."
   b. Goal: "I want to lose 5 pounds per month every month this year."

3. **Goals are attainable.** This does not mean we want to eliminate God's power from our lives. It simply means that you will not be able to control the outcome of impossible dreams. Goals should be God-sized, but written in a way that He will equip you. Everything above that God does is great – it just can't fit in the goal category.
   a. Dream: "I want my son to be a professional bowler."
   b. Goal: "I want my son to have at least one regular exercise habit that he enjoys by the time he leaves home."

DREAMS ARE NOT ENEMIES OF GOALS

Dreams are wonderful to have around. As a dreamer myself, I understand the joy of asking "why not?" and the importance of expecting great things from God. This is not contradictory to the goal setting we are about to embark on. In fact, this should enhance the whole process! Knowing that God can do "immeasurably more than all we could ask or imagine" should make our pursuit that much more of an adventure.

4. **Goals have a deadline.** Every goal you set must have a completion date in mind. Otherwise, it is just a wish. That is exactly why it is necessary to have three sets of goals:

- **Lifetime goals** to accomplish before we die.

- **Long term goals** to accomplish in the next 5-10 years.

- **Short-term goals** to accomplish in six months or less.

Obviously, you could have every measure of time in-between. But practically speaking, these three deadlines will allow you to set shorter goals that stem from larger goals – allowing yourself a greater opportunity for success.

    a. Dream: "Some day I want to get a Master's degree.

    b. Goal: "I want to get a Master's Degree in the next five years."

5. **Goals are written down.** This is obvious enough that I will not insult your intelligence with an example!

THE BIG SWITCH

And now, a surprise! We have established the five key roles in which goals need to be established and defined how effective goals are formulated. Before we go on, a MAJOR TRANSITION needs to happen.

From this point forward in the "Direction" section, we will cease to talk about the abstract roles and begin speaking of the people in our lives. **After all, people are the only aspect of this world that will move into eternity. Would it not make sense that we invest our *limited* time on the thing that will be impacted for *unlimited* time? Jesus invested His life in people – not schedules, ideas, issues, or things. People and relationships should receive our strongest focus.**

Look back on your "five starters," and next to each one, identify the individuals in your life that are impacted by each of those five roles. Some will be obvious. Next to "husband," I'll write my wife's name, and next to "father" I will write in Ryley and Reagan – my daughters' names. Some are less obvious. If you have "Employee," for example, you may write down the names of your boss and subordinates.

This will make a tremendous difference as we go forward.

There is no greater role model in history than Jesus Christ, and the Word of God gives us a glimpse into areas in which He developed during His life on earth. These

> "Do not be content with being average. Average is as close to the bottom as it is to the top."
>
> Anon.

four areas give us a tremendous example to follow as we formulate our goals:

> "And Jesus grew in wisdom and stature, and in favor with God and men" (Luke 2:52).

This one powerful summary of Jesus' human development defines what we will call our "Goal Quadrant:"

THE GOAL QUADRANT	
Mind Goals	Body Goals
God Goals	People Goals

The Goal Quadrant

1. **Mind Goals ("Wisdom")** – We need to define the ways in which we will continue to grow in knowledge and education. We have information available every day that can help us better anticipate the challenges before us and move ahead wisely.

2. **Body Goals ("Stature")** – We need to define the ways we will honor God with our temples. Our physical maintenance will have an impact on every other area of our lives. Medical science has continually proven that physical conditioning impacts our emotions and mental stamina. More importantly, the Bible indicates that self-discipline in the form of physical exertion also impacts our spiritual walk.

> "We make a living by what we get; we make a life by what we give."
> Winston Churchill

3. **God Goals ("Favor with God")** – Defining where we want to be in our spiritual walk and how we intend to get there is essential to joyful living.

4. **People Goals ("Favor with...Men")** – This is speaking of working toward influence and respect among those God places in your path. I believe this quadrant needs to be broken down into three specific categories that are spoken of in Scripture. **These people are all involved in an emotional transaction with me in my life.** I will use an "S&L" acrostic to illustrate the healthy transactions in each category.

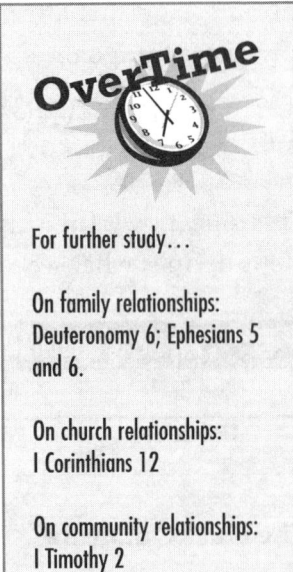

For further study...

On family relationships:
Deuteronomy 6; Ephesians 5 and 6.

On church relationships:
I Corinthians 12

On community relationships:
I Timothy 2

   a. **Family** – those people related to you by marriage or birth. God has given you specific commands to grow in this area.

      ■ **"S&L Transaction"** – Safety and Legacy. Home is ordained to be a place of protection, and also a place where core values are cultivated and passed on to future generations.

"Tis easier to prevent bad habits than to break them."
                                    Benjamin Franklin

b. **Church** – As a Christian, I am called to be part of a larger family of people as well. This group also brings new opportunities and responsibilities directed by God. If you are not part of a church, I encourage you once again to review chapter five, "The Greatest News in the Entire Book"

- ■ **"S&L Transaction"** – **Service and Love.** This God-ordained group of people is so special, He calls it "The Body of Christ." As a part of this body, we are called to the joy of serving one another and of reflecting Christ's unconditional love and grace.

c. **Community** – This is everyone with whom I have contact and influence. As an American, this includes government leaders. I have an influence on who serves in office and for how long.

- ■ **"S&L Transaction"** – **Salt and Light.** I have a responsibility to impact those around me with the joy and peace I have found in Christ. I have the opportunity to make a difference for eternity in the lives of my coworkers, neighbors, and friends, through my words and actions.

LET'S PRETEND YOU'RE DEAD!
(A LOOK AT LIFETIME GOALS)

Perhaps you have already begun to formulate the three key elements in your life that you want to be remembered for when you are gone, but we'll put them on hold for a moment.

Trick Yourself!

When breaking down bigger tasks into smaller ones, think of each task as its own project. Sometimes that helps you ease your stress load about the massiveness of the final goal. It works for me!

In fact, your hopes about what your life's accomplishments are completely unimportant right now – because we are going to pretend you are dead. BOOM – you just hit the floor like a rock. Family and friends are gathering to grieve the loss and to remember the good times. The ones you knew best will now have the responsibility to outline to the rest of the world why your life was significant. As they begin to write the obituary, they must summarize two or three key elements that embodied your life. What was so special about your short time here?

Obviously, your loved ones will be kind in their wording. But let us consider for a moment they were interested ONLY in honesty and extreme accuracy in their assessment of your life. How might they fill in the following?

> "Time sneaks up on you like a windshield on a bug."
> — Jon Lithgow

_____, passed from this life just the other day. He left behind _____.

He spent the bulk of his/her time engulfed in his passion for: _____.

If you talked to those who knew him, they would tell you that the most important thing in his life was his devotion to _____ .

Often _____ made great sacrifices to make time for his other love,_____.
Many, many hours of love and sacrifice went toward strengthening this area of his life.

Family members said he had always dreamed of doing more _____, but never really found the time to develop this passion more fully.

In lieu of flowers, the family feels that _____ would rather have you send money to the following: _____.
They feel certain this is where he would want gifts to go because of how important it was to him in life.

And so ends the obituary. If you are like me, that little experiment can be painful. I am thankful that, at least today, I have been given the opportunity to revise the contents of my legacy. Still, this brings up an important point. If you are not doing what you want to be doing then...What do you need to be doing?

That is what's so great about goal-setting! We can rebuild and refine our current obituaries. We get to correct those points in the obituary that were difficult to swallow. This time, imagine the "best case scenario." All the things you really care about will be reflected in what people saw of your life.

With that in mind, let's start again:

God-Pleasers Vs. World-Teasers

In I Samuel 8:1-22, the children of Israel had it all — God was their king and the Promised Land was their home. Admittedly, there were certainly some problems — Samuel's sons were corrupt, and the elders of Israel wanted to make things better. But surprisingly, the solution they chose to remedy the problem was where they went astray.

Rather than go to the King of Kings for their needs, they sought a human answer in a human king. The Lord gave them what they wanted, and His people suffered for generations because of their quest to be like all of the other nations.

As the world around us becomes more and more degraded, it seems our goal as Christians has moved from being God-pleasers to simply trying to be a little better than the world. As a result, most believers can track a parallel between our own spiritual decline and that of the culture around us. We have sought to rise above the world rather than to rest in God's unchanging standard.

If we want our homes to please our Father, we have to first learn to ignore what "all the other nations" are doing, and get back to pleasing the only one that matters.

_____, passed from this life just the other day. He left behind _____.

He spent the bulk of his/her time engulfed in his passion for: _____.

If you talked to those who knew him, they would tell you that the most important thing in his life was his devotion to _____ .

Often _____ made great sacrifices to make time for his other love, _____. Many, many hours of love and sacrifice went toward strengthening this area of his life.

Family members said he had always dreamed of doing more _____, but never really found the time to develop this passion more fully.

In lieu of flowers, the family feels that _____ would rather have you send money to the following: _____. They feel certain this is where he would want gifts to go because of how important it was to him in life.

With that rather morbid exercise behind us, we have taken the first step in writing down our goals. **You have just revealed your lifetime goals – the essence of what you want to accomplish before you die.** It is out of these core goals that you will build goals for the long- and short-term. As you write, keep in mind that these are an outpouring of the people affected by your principle roles in life, and they should fit in all four of the "goal quadrants" of life.

My wife and I have been planning a big RV trip. We have never RV'd before, and in seeking out that perfect inaugural destination, we sometimes get carried away. It is far too easy to look at a map and say, "We could cut across here and take in this other destination on the way home. It is only two inches out of the way." Those two inches are a "mere" 500 miles, and will certainly be a big deal when the trip comes around! Likewise, you cannot have every destination in mind when you answer the critical question of your lifetime goals. This is your ultimate calling in life. You cannot have too many goals and expect to reach all of them. Lifetime goals are the framework for the remaining components of this workbook. You may end up adjusting these to some extent, but it will be a great help if you have a strong feeling about these before moving forward.

LONG-TERM GOALS

Short-term goals are there to support long-term goals. It would stand to reason, then, that we must establish our long-term goals before moving on. As a reminder, these long-term goals are things you want to accomplish in the next five to ten years. These may be tied to very specific, pre-determined dates:

> "There is a time when one must firmly choose the course we will follow or the endless drift of events will make the decision for us."
> H.V. Prochnow

- A child's graduation from high school. ("I want to help my daughters memorize two books of the Bible before they graduate from high school.")

- A "milestone" birthday. ("I want to attain a Master's Degree before my fortieth birthday.")

- A date that is financially or mathematically predictable. ("I want to purchase a house in exactly five years.")

Others may not be tied to specific dates, but a specific date is still a great thing to assign and aim for.

SHORT-TERM GOALS

The first step to writing your short-term goals is to break down your long-term goals into specific, attainable tasks. This step will determine whether you ever reach your lifetime goals. These should be realistic and specific.

Short-term goals also have another unique characteristic that will become critical as we move into the next section of our text: these goals are the first ones to show up on the calendar. Short-term goals will be broken down into small tasks so that they can be assigned to specific actions in the immediate future. As a result, these short-term goals quickly become several one-day and one-week goals.

This is great news, because now we can begin seeing

> "The best time to make a decision is before you have to make one."
> **Nelson Price**

results as we move toward our primary purposes in life!

Setting a Standard

God has given us three key elements by which to measure our lives:

- **The Law of God delineates much of the so-called "gray area" in our society today.** Oftentimes the issues society pretends to be uncertain about are clearly defined in the Word of God. We can no more ignore these standards without natural consequences than we could ignore the law of gravity when jumping out of a tall building.

- **The lessons of God go even deeper than the Law itself.** Much of Jesus' Sermon on the Mount was devoted to expounding on Old Testament law – moving beyond the precepts of God to the principles behind them. From Jesus' teaching, we know that it would be futile to look for "loopholes" in His law. First of all, there are none. Secondly, we are called to honor not only His commands but also the principles behind those commands.

- **The Lord Himself is our ultimate standard.** When making a difficult decision, we must always ask ourselves, "How would this action be a reflection of who God is?" Secondly, we must ask if those actions will ultimately glorify Him, even if we find no specific prohibition in His law.

The standards God has set for us will establish the direction in which we should be headed as our goals are written down.

It would be irresponsible of us to lay out a course for our lives with the assumption that any old course will do. God has outlined a specific path for us to follow, and that should be the foundation for our goals and dreams.

> **Close2Home**
>
>
>
> How Full is the Cup These Days — or How Empty?
>
> Perspective can make a tremendous difference in your ability to get things done. Shifting your focus from the negative to the positive can give you a "can-do" attitude that will make you far more productive.
>
> "Never forget that all you have is all you need." — Sarah Ban Breathnach

We live in a society where many live as if there is no absolute truth:

"If it feels good, do it!"

"What's right for you may not be right for me."

Indeed, if you asked many Americans, they would willingly volunteer that their most valued attribute is "tolerance." This means they are willing to accept anyone's behavior as "right" if the person is comfortable with the way he or she is living.

> "Try not to become a person of success but rather a person of value."
> Albert Einstein

In fact, it is impossible to press forward in striving for the holiness God commands until we re-establish this important truth in our lives.

SEEK HIM FIRST!

Many things we work on every day are not the most important things in our lives. We put aside what is important and focus on insignificant things that fill up our time. Can you name something you have done in the past few days that really didn't matter at all?

The Bible gives us a very simple solution for getting our priorities in order – SEEK HIM FIRST! When we seek God first every day, the rest of our time begins to take on more importance. When we are in the process of serving a magnificent God, we will never be satisfied with focusing on the temporal things of life.

As you begin putting your goals together, ask yourself how many of your priorities really have God's best interests at heart.

One thing we often forget about time is that we need to think about more than just minutes, days, or even years. We need to think about ETERNITY. The fact is that every person on this earth will live forever in eternity in one of two places. One of them is wonderful. The terrible alternative is seldom discussed, but real and dreadful all the same.

> "One main test of our dealings with the world is whether the men and women we associate with are better or worse for it."
> George MacDonald

The Bible says Hell is a place far away from God, and that it is a lonely, painful, sad, and terrible place to spend even one second – much less forever! Many have asked, in fact, how a loving God could send people there. We must always remember that a person chooses hell by denying God's invitation to heaven.

We must never forget that "God has set eternity in the hearts of men" (Ecclesiastes 3:11), and there is a longing in every heart for heaven. One of Satan's greatest strategies is to minimize the beauty of the place. As Randy Alcorn wrote in his book *In Light of Eternity*, "After being forcefully evicted from Heaven (Isaiah 14:12-15), the devil is bitter not only toward God, but toward us and the place that's no longer his. It must be maddening to Satan to realize we are now entitled to the home he was kicked out of. What better way for demons to attack than to whisper lies about the very place God tells us to set our hearts and minds on?"

As different as they may be, both heaven and hell are as real as where you are sitting right now. Live today as if you are investing for the next million years.

Taming the Thieves

In the insecure world we call home, alarm systems can be found on houses everywhere. Most prudent residents would not think of going to bed without a double-locked door. We go to great lengths to protect the ones we love!

Would you even think of allowing thieves free reign over your home and family on a daily basis? While it seems

Close2Home

How's Your Report Card?

Your kids get report cards. Why should you be different? Document your progress on a weekly basis to help keep you motivated.

Teachers use skills checklists to "check off" the progress of their students. By doing the same for yourself, you will be able to easily see what you have accomplished and what needs improvement.

unthinkable, most of us miss the "petty thieves" that make their way right through the front door.

In the Near East a shepherd often slept in the entrance of the fold to guard his sheep. Thus Jesus watches over His own. Yet as gatekeepers of our own flocks, we are warned that the thief's motives are always worse than they might appear – to steal, to kill, and to destroy – and we must stay alert to their presence.

Take a mental walk through your home. Do you have anything that could rob you of your joy? Of a closer walk with God? Is there anything that could steal the hearts and minds of your children?

Common thieves to watch out for:
- Television programs
- Worldly Attitudes
- Magazines and books
- Compromises in your own integrity
- Music

As moms and dads, we must stay "on alert" for the covert operations of the enemy! **There is not room for even**

one wolf in the flock of an effective shepherd. We cannot afford to make excuses.

SPEED UP OR SLOW DOWN?

As parents sometimes it is tough to find God's balance in the area of planning for the future. It seems so much easier to throw our problems over our shoulders and plunge ahead rather than to stop and ask God for directions.

It seems that most of us fall into two extremes when it comes to this issue:

- **We Ignore Where God Says to Go.** Sometimes it is all too obvious which direction we need to go in certain areas of life, and yet we hesitate. We overspiritualize our inaction by telling ourselves that we are waiting to hear from God. Is there something that God has already made clear to you on which you have yet to take action?

- **We Count On Ourselves.** All too often we try to "go it alone" - boldly believing that we can forge our own spiritual path without the Lord's guidance. More often than not, this results in failure or frustration.

BUILD SOME BIGGER GOALS!

It is believed that the sun burns up more energy in one second than mankind has utilized in all of human history. And that is just one of the countless stars placed in the heavens by our omnipotent God! We often forget the magnitude – the absolute bigness – of the God we serve. The evidence of God's power is all around us, but here are two key exhibits:

- **His Creation** – Everywhere we turn, if we open our eyes a little wider, we can see amazing evidence of what God has created in His power and wisdom.

- **The Power of the Son** – Jesus has demonstrated power over nature, sickness, death, and demons. He constantly shows Himself to be all-powerful.

This same God tells us continually throughout His word that He wants to share that power with those who follow Him. And yet, today so many believers are powerless and victimized. Dr. Rick Warren has said, "God has given us atomic bomb power, and we live firecracker lives." Most of us have never really grasped the extent of the help that God has to offer us as we do His work. Are we really setting God-sized goals in our lives, or are we setting safer goals we might be able to pull off on our own?

God wants to give you the power to get started and the power to keep going. We must look intently at His Word and pray for wisdom in trusting God for big things.

Scripture does not say that we should not plan – Paul continually shared his goals for the coming days in his writings – but it does say we should plan with a spirit of prayer, humility, and trust. This comes from realizing how quickly things can change and counting only on God's provision and protection.

NO MORE SIGHS

The final illustration that Moses grants us in these first eleven verses of Psalm 90 is that of a person looking back on his or her life with a sigh of regret. Regret is what comes from a knowledge of what should have been with the recognition that it is too late to do anything about it now. Most of us can look back at some portion of our lives and wish for a "do-over," but that is the challenge of time itself. We can never go backwards.

It is interesting that a major theme of science fiction films over the years has been time-travel – the ability to travel backward to some moment of years past, or quickly move forward to some time in the distant future. In fact, we all get to enjoy time-travel, but the speed is just not space age enough to entertain us. We experience time-travel every day of our lives, and we will never be here again. That is why the regrets seem to hurt so much. The death of a loved one brings thoughts of missed opportunities and words not spoken. Regrets can eat away at us, and can cause even more trouble. In dwelling on past failures, we end up missing out on current opportunities – causing a vicious cycle of despair that can end up robbing us of whatever life we have left.

To illustrate the point of what regrets can do in our lives, let's return with Moses to Mt. Sinai in Exodus 3. Moses approaches the burning bush and is called by God. He responds to God by saying, "Here I am." As God outlines the plan for Moses, he fires back with question after question indicating he has serious doubts about his own ability to lead the Israelites anywhere – much less out of the grip of Pharaoh. Moses more than anyone knew the power of Pharaoh's regime to stop such a movement. Moses had forty years earlier demonstrated a deep, moving concern for his Jewish brethren, and surely he had suffered many regrets over four decades, wondering what could have been if he had responded wisely to the Egyptian confrontation that led to the murder resulting in his exile.

Moses was telling God why he was inadequate and incapable of what God was calling him to do. God's response to Moses in each account was a different version of this paraphrased response: "You do not have to do it. I will do it through you." Moses' shame and regret had left him with a feeling of inadequacy.

There is always a postscript to the regret Moses is speaking of. That special message for us is II Corinthians 5:17: "Therefore, if any man is in Christ, he is a new creature; the old things passed away, behold all things have become new." Our God is the God of the second chance. He allows us the privilege of starting where we are, and not where we should be. God has given us a very special gift that is probably the best kept secret among time management tools. The gift of contentment is the underlying theme of our most important lesson on time:
Because of the Cross, we do not have the responsibility of seeking to undo all of the mistakes we have made in the past. We have the undeserved privilege of starting right where we are in our quest toward productive living.

GUARD YOUR GARDEN!

Several years ago, I planted a garden with my kids thinking it would be a great way to illustrate the principles of sowing and reaping. After we tilled a small patch of ground in the backyard, however, things started going awry. Our first mistake was letting the kids plant any and every type of seed they wanted to see grow. We planted some twenty-five different plants in a 3-by-6 plot of land. As you can tell, I'm no gardener!

After three weeks, it was very exciting to see all of the sprouts rising up from the earth. But after three months, we had a full-blown jungle in the back corner of our yard; And when the time came to harvest, every plant had either been choked to death or eaten by rabbits.

Needless to say, my reaping lesson was laid to waste. In its place I learned another one – if you try to plant everything, what really matters will be crowded out by things that are less important. And so it goes with our goals. If we try to do everything we will end up with absolutely nothing of value to show for our efforts.

Choose your direction wisely. It will one day become your legacy.

CHAPTER THREE

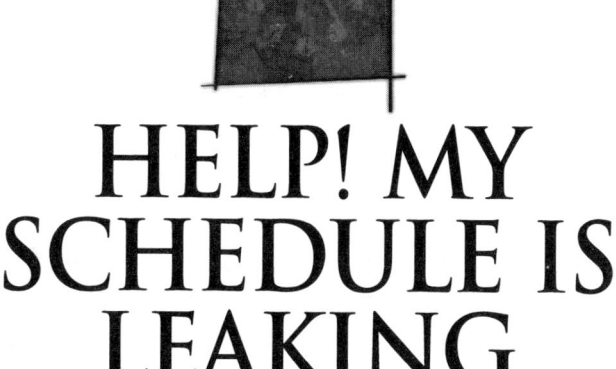

HELP! MY SCHEDULE IS LEAKING

THE POWER OF PLANNING

A few months ago while traveling in Virginia, I was invited to dinner at the home of some friends. They had actually invited several friends and family members over to celebrate a birthday. When I arrived at the house, I noticed right away that something was not quite right. Everyone in the house was frantically moving furniture and ripping away at the carpeting. Not quite the birthday celebration that I expected!

It turns out that the lady of the house had gone in to take a bath about two hours before my arrival. Right after she started the bath water, the phone rang. She spent the next forty-five minutes on the phone with an old friend as the water continued to run.

Repairmen estimated that at least 200 gallons of water had escaped into the house during that period of time. What surprised me most was not the amount of water in the bathroom and hall – where you might expect it to travel, but the unlikely places where the water crept. It traveled through walls and flooring to literally saturate the entire home. We continued to find new places water had traveled throughout the night. I spoke with them about four weeks after the incident. They were having to install all-new flooring in both the bottom floor and basement of their home!

You will notice right away that no names were used in this story. The woman pleaded with me to not reveal her identity, but the story was just too good to leave out! I learned a critical lesson about time management that evening.

The Average American Will Spend...

*One year looking for misplaced objects
*Eight months opening junk mail
*Six months sitting at stoplights
*2 years unsuccessfully returning phone calls
*4 years doing housework
*5 years waiting in line
*6 years eating

(U.S. News and World Report, Jan. 30, 1989, p. 81, survey of 6000 people polled in 1988)

Time, like water, is very difficult to control when it is outside of an organized system.

Water is an integral part of nearly every home, but when it loses boundaries, it can be the home's undoing. Likewise, our home life can grow chaotic in a big hurry when calendar events overflow. There is one major difference, though. Unlike water, when your time overflows, you cannot undo past damage when time has been ignored.

Planning is the plumbing of our home organization. It keeps calendars in check, creates places for enjoyment, and helps us eliminate unwanted waste in life (I tried to be as gentle as possible with that analogy!) It is also where most of the attention in time management needs to be focused. The essence of our "plan for planning" is this:

By giving substance to my schedule, I can place my desired actions in a logical sequence, thereby gaining a realistic chance for success.

Moses Gives us the "How To"

Now we get to the heart of our study! As Moses reaches verse 12 in the ninetieth Psalm, he makes a major transition from the desolate picture of the previous verses to the core of his time management philosophy:

> "Teach us to number our days aright, that
> we may gain a heart of wisdom."

With this one verse, we have everything we need to build a successful time management system.

> "It is not enough to be busy...the question is: What are we busy about?"
> Henry David Thoreau

Here are the three key components:

Component One: A Teachable Spirit. ("Teach us") Moses makes the request with a teachable heart. This one-hundred-something-year-old-man was asking God to continue advising him about the mysteries of time. Like Moses, we should begin our scheduling process by asking God to reveal things to us we might be blind to otherwise. The closer you get to God, the more productive your schedule will become!

Component Two: A Simple, Specific Calendar. ("number our days") We need to specify and quantify the time we spend. By numbering our days, we give them a measurable substance. By maintaining a simple, manageable calendar, we can identify weak spots and make our goals a reality. When we begin to quantify our time and view it based on the events attached to it, we can begin planning more efficiently and effectively with less wasted effort.

Component Three: Sound Judgment. ("that we may gain a heart of wisdom") Ultimately, efficient management of the calendar leads to an ability to make sound, wise decisions. Moses is contending that the ability to "number our days" will lead to greater wisdom in our walk through life. At its very core, time management is nothing more than a continued series of decisions. Unfortunately, most people make important decisions in everyday life flippantly. With wisdom, decisions are made

> "Worry does not empty tomorrow of it's sorrow; it empties today of it's strength."
>
> Corrie Ten Boom

based on a well thought-out plan and a set of core values.

These three essential components create the heart of the system we introduce now. In my seminars, **I am often asked which calendar company or tool I recommend.** There are so many on the market today – Franklin-Covey ©, Daytimer ©, DayRunner ©, and Cambridge ©. Then there are the electronic tools – I-Paqs ©, Palms ©, and on the list goes. I placed copyright symbols there for legal reasons, of course. But I also wanted to make a point. I am going to let you in on a little secret:

They are all the same.

That's right! In its essence, the management of time needs only to consist of two components:

- **A list of tasks:** the flexible portion of a schedule and

- **A calendar on which those tasks are assigned a time:** the specific portion of the schedule.

For the sake of argument, I'll throw in one more key component that is almost essential, but only if you have papers you need to keep with you:

- **A filing system to store frequently used information:** the storage portion of the schedule.

> "Just as there are no little people or unimportant lives, there is no insignificant work."
>
> Elena Bonner

No matter how the above brands are broken down, they all have these three attributes as a common denominator. **My point is this – it is not the tool you choose, but it is how you *use* the tool you choose!** I have met owners of all of the above who are as disorganized as you can possibly imagine. On the other hand, some of the most organized people I have ever known use a two-dollar calendar and a legal pad to map out their lives.

Close2Home

Don't Pass the Buck Just Yet

It is not unusual in family life to find yourself stuck with a task or responsibility you never really wanted to do. The first option in this situation is normally to look for a way of delegating the task, but there may be a far better way to handle it. Keep in mind that others are trying to manage their calendars as well!

Perhaps a better alternative would be to throw out the task or responsibility completely. If it is not worth your time and attention, then it may not be worth anyone's time!

Unfortunately, when most people want to get organized, they head straight for the office supply store and purchase a $100 leather-bound "planning station" thinking that it will solve all of their problems. Unfortunately, most often it only leaves them with a nice looking leather notebook that put them $100 in debt. Before you buy ANYTHING, read these key steps to successful planning. I do not purport these to be the end-all of planning knowledge, or even the one-and-only Biblical way to plan. These are, however, the result of extensive research, and a combination of methods used by hundreds of successful time managers in nearly every walk of life.

Another key component you will notice right away is the "launching point" for the planning process. Most planning systems mention that you ought to include family in your calendar. This is usually mentioned as an aside. It is simply something to be done at the end of the day – after all of the important tasks have been completed. Ironically, most Americans believe their family is of utmost importance in their lives, but those same families are the last item to be included on a planning calendar. The Home on Time system will show you a realistic way to accomplish your goals in life by beginning with family priorities.

> **"FAMILY F.I.L.M."** –
> Family Summit,
> Focus Time,
> Identify Immovables,
> List Tasks,
> Map the Calendar

A Logical Game Plan for a Family-Friendly Calendar

Lana and I are not big moviegoers – primarily because we tend to be homebodies. Given a night of freedom, we both prefer to stay home and sit back with a pair of good books, or a movie on video. To me, one of the great things about watching movies at home is you can carry on an open dialogue during the film. I tend to look for areas of a movie that are not as realistic as they should be. I am sort of the Hollywood version of the armchair quarterback. "There is no way he could have gotten there in time! This movie is ridiculous," I might proclaim, with all my filmmaking wisdom and experience. It is always at these points that

> *"To be happy at home is the end of all labor."*
> Samuel Johnson

Lana will chime in with her role as the "shusher" – telling me to be quiet and watch – and give her familiar retort to my reactions, "Ryan, it's a movie. It's not supposed to be realistic!" Most would agree that movies are full of actions and events that cannot occur in real life. The actors are always ready with just the right profound statement or karate kick to solve the problem at hand. They are prepared, of course, because a group of writers has spent hours at a conference table thinking up just the right move each person ought to make. In essence, the difference is planning.

Heritage Builders, a ministry of Focus on the Family™, has developed a whole line of products to help you develop successful family times. For more information, check out www.heritagebuilders.com!

We will never be able to script our lives so that everything works out in a neat, two-hour package, but we can certainly learn something from the methods used in scripting a film. Just like moviemakers, we are attempting each day to create a documentary of our lives that will make as positive an impact as possible. The nuts and bolts of planning a daily calendar are much the same as the fundamentals of writing. Keep this in mind as I lay out a very simple plan to be used every day in your quest for greater productivity.

> "Dost thou love life? Then do not squander time, for that is the stuff life is made of."
> — Benjamin Franklin

In some ways, planning is just the opposite of responding. As we know by now, in responding, you are seeking to anticipate and adapt to uncontrollable forces, but in planning, you are seeking to gain as much control of the day's events as possible. And it is in this planning process that we carry our film-writing analogy to it's most practical point. In making films, the producer must follow some basic steps to end up with an excellent product that goes to market. We'll use the acrostic "Family F.I.L.M." to help us remember these essentials.

How Did Jesus Manage Time?

For some insight into how Jesus managed time during His ministry, try a study through the book of Mark. Note what prompted Him to move on to another endeavor, what steps He took to spend time in prayer, and ways He responded to situations when they took place.

Of course, we are producing a "Family Film" in our own effort, so before we dive into the acrostic, we have to include a Family Element up front.

Step One: Family Summit. This is a time for the entire family that takes place once a week. For most families, Sunday afternoon or evening is a great time to begin this weekly tradition, and it will become something your family looks forward to if done correctly. The Family Summit has three key goals.

> "Do what you can, with what you have, where you are."
> **Theodore Roosevelt**

- **First, you want to synchronize your schedules,** so that time spent together through the week is maximized, important events are highlighted on all individual calendars, and nothing essential is passed by.

- **Secondly, you want to talk.** That may sound over-simplified, but many families go weeks on end without any meaningful conversation. This step can be as basic as throwing out a topic of discussion and asking each family member to chime in on their feelings. In the end, you will want to talk about what Scripture has to say about the topic at hand.

- **Finally, the Family Summit is a time to pray.** Prayer as a family usually takes place around the dinner table if at all, and is often lost to the business of home life any other time. Maintain an ongoing list of prayer needs mentioned by each family member, and review God's answers to those prayers as you continue to meet in coming weeks.

Step Two: Focus Time. Nothing of significance can ever be accomplished apart from a logical game plan, and this starts with a focus time. Our Savior Jesus Christ was often found removing Himself from the hustle and bustle of life to steal away for a time of prayer and focus. If He needed such a time, how much more do we? **You should have a time *every day* in which you are reflecting on past efforts and looking toward the next twenty-four hours.** Jesus told us to live life one day at a time, and we should take that literally. This would also be a great time to begin meeting with God in prayer and devotions. If you are already doing so, I would recommend that you tack on your planning session to that time. Remember – the first component of healthy planning is a teachable spirit, and that comes from a prayerful heart.

Would you be willing to give up twenty minutes of your day if it would guarantee you an additional three hours of saved time? That's a minimum of what you can look forward to in exchange for this small investment. Mark your calendar now for this essential step.

Step Three: Identify "Immovables" in Your Schedule. We all have some areas in our calendars that we cannot move without some major consequences. For obvious reasons, these are the first segments of life that need to be reflected on your calendar. We will surround the other essentials of life around these pillars. Depending on your key roles, these immovables may include job-related meetings, school times, church activities, holidays, and sleep. Sleep is one of the most underrated immovables we deal with in life. Be sure that your schedule allows for it, or it will come back to haunt you later!

By the end of your focus time each morning, every one of these "immovables" should be solidly indicated on your calendar. **While we cannot control the fact that the "immovables" have to happen, we do often have the ability to make them more predictable.** We have the

> "The whole point of getting things done is knowing what to leave undone."
> Oswald Chambers

power to determine the time these tasks and responsibilities will take place. If that is the case, do everything you can to place these immovables in a regular time slot in regular intervals.

This process helps shed some light on my preference for calendar formats. Given the choice, I prefer a page-per-week format as shown on the opposite page. By lining up the days of the week where corresponding times are parallel, you can map out one slot all week for immovable tasks. This creates a sense of predictability in the planning process, and helps you stay on task.

Step Four: List Tasks you would like to complete. The tasks listed at this point are in no particular order and have no specific deadline in mind. They are simply a culmination of all you would like to do. However, you will want to begin this process with your short- and long-term goals in full view. These goals should dictate much of what you desire to do. **This is not the time to evaluate order of priority or qualification, but simply a chance to write down everything.** As you continue these daily focus times, this process will not need to be repeated fully. You will be building off of your initial list.

Once the list is on paper, the fun begins! At this point, many planners on the market today challenge users to assign either an "A," "B," or "C" priority to each task – demonstrating the urgency of its completion. In other words, A's need to be done first, B's next, C's if you get

---

| Excellence is not an act… but a habit. – Aristotle |

around to it. I see two major flaws with this system, however:

- By assigning essential tasks to be done today with an "A," you are no closer to accomplishing the task. You have not done what really helps get an essential task accomplished, which is assigning a logical first step to that task.

Close2Home

Busy Kids

Today's teens — and even pre-teens are busier than ever. It would have been totally ridiculous just a few years ago to see kids with daily planners or digital assistants at school, but today it is a necessity. Recent studies indicate that teens are spending 6-10 hours a week on homework alone! All of these scheduling rigors can take a toll on a young person already dealing with the stress of just growing up.

At the same time, studies show that kids who are involved are normally better citizens. So how can parents strike a balance? Here are just a couple of tips that parents have shared:

- A major priority as parents is to create opportunities for our kids to experience success. That means identifying their strengths and helping them capitalize on them. Once you find the things your teen truly enjoys and in which he or she excels, help them to focus there.

- Once the strong points are identified, encourage kids to focus on just a few things to do well. While there may be merit on being a four-sport letterman and colleges may be impressed by a full slate of campus club affiliations, the tradeoff may be mediocrity in all of them. Focusing on key extracurricular activities can really remove a lot of the pressure and help kids excel.

- "C" tasks are not worth the ink with which they are written. By assigning something a "C," you are saying, "This is a non-essential task that would be nice to get done today if it happens to work out perfectly. If not, it doesn't matter." Who has ever completed a "C" task? A better alternative would be to assign this task in a time or day where you will have the freedom to complete it.

Step Five: Map the Calendar. Now we have the information we need to go forward with mapping out your process. The term "mapping" is the best picture of what you will be doing next, because you are going to write down directions for yourself to get where you want to go. This word-picture also helps us answer an important question:

How much detail do I need to include in my daily planner?

The answer is the same as it would be if you were driving somewhere and you were mapping out directions. **You need as much information as you need to get you to your destination, but no more.** Additionally, you may need a more detailed map the first few times you go on a trip to a new city, but after making the trip a few times, you need only jot down the basics of the journey. The rest will happen almost automatically.

Mapping the calendar is the process of assigning a place

> "One never notices what has been done; one can only see what remains to be done."
> Madame Curie

for each task you have outlined. There are two steps in this process:

1. **First, identify the essential tasks for a given day.** These tasks need to be assigned a specific time in which to get done. If a task absolutely has to get done, it deserves a block of time on the schedule – not a note out to the side of the schedule. Some essential tasks do not have to be done today, but have a deadline in the future. Go ahead and assign them a time on the schedule at some future date.

Look for Combos that Work for You

At the time of this writing, I use a Palm PDA for daily tasks and appointments, as well as to hold all of my phone numbers and addresses. I then combine it with a basic paper planner featuring an "A-Z" tabbed file system for notes and essential documents, printed versions of my month-at-a-glance calendar, and a notepad.

This allows me to have only one place to input my calendar information so nothing falls through the cracks. It also gives me the freedom to handwrite notes to be entered in the PDA at a more convenient time of the day. I find this combination gives me maximum efficiency through the day, and keeps my data loss extremely low. That is the key you will need to find in the system that works for you.

2. Not every task deserves a time slot. **The second step is maintaining a list of these flexible tasks so that they can be readily available,** when appointed tasks are completed early. In other words, the tasks that must be done today (what

some call the "A" tasks,) do not even show up on your daily task list. They show up on your daily calendar.

Pardon Me, Mr. Task. Do You Have a Reservation?

Last Valentine's Day, I took my wife and girls out to a very nice restaurant downtown. We invited along a close friend, and as it turned out, this ended up being a great move. The restaurant did not take reservations for parties under five. Because of the holiday, the place was jam-packed, but we walked right in and went straight to our table. Most of the people were there as couples – because of the holiday – and they had to wait in line to be served. Some of the same people waiting when we arrived were still waiting when we left two hours later!

That is the best picture I can think of between "A-Tasks" and "B-Tasks": Your high-priority tasks are given a reservation on the calendar, while your next-priority tasks simply have to wait in line.

The "Family F.I.L.M." process takes the basic elements of the best planning systems I have seen and makes them easily attainable. It gives you the greatest opportunity possible for achieving success. This simple shell offers all the components you need, but do not get too excited just yet.

Beware of the Organization Impostors

There are still opportunities to fail miserably. I have come

> "You will never 'find' time for anything. If you want time, you must make it."
> Charles Buxton

across many people over the years who have the best planning systems money can buy and plan out each of their days with precision, but are still frustrated with limited productivity at the end of the day. **There are still some traps we can fall into that might look a lot like healthy organization – until they expose themselves for what they really are when it is too late to turn back.** The following represent the top five "organization impostors" I have found in our culture today:

What is That Doing Here?

Before anything goes on your calendar, you should be able to give a positive response to one of these two questions:

- Do I need to do this task? Or
- Do I want to do this task?

If it is not helping you reach your lifetime goals and you do not enjoy it, get the task off of your calendar!

1. **Calendar Addiction.** Some people I know have calendars plastered on a wall in every room of their homes, one in their wallets, one on their desk at work, and two in the car that were given to them by well-meaning salesmen. They feel very secure in knowing they have worked so hard to be aware of the time, but never really know what time it is at all. They will often write down an appointment on

> "You will find, as you look back upon your life, that the moments when you have really lived are the moments when you have done things in the spirit of love."
>
> Henry Drummond

the calendar closest at hand, hoping when the event comes up they will happen to look in that particular calendar. They constantly miss appointments and deadlines because they dropped the ball while juggling all those calendars.

There is nothing noble or efficient about having more than one calendar. Confusion does not make anyone more organized. I am not even a fan of having one central family calendar on the refrigerator door, because things still get passed by. If families are synchronizing activities during the Family Summit, these extra calendars are not necessary.

2. **"Dream – Planning."** If you were to count up the estimated time it takes to complete the average person's to-do list, you would find enough tasks to span more than twenty-four hours. Many of us find ourselves overloading the daily to-do list in hopes that somehow today we will accomplish more than we ever have in our entire lives. Of course, this never happens. It only leaves us frustrated with more to do tomorrow.

A good rule of thumb in this area is to schedule for one-third less in your day than you feel you can accomplish. This will allow more time than you had planned for specific tasks because they always

---

"Some things are very important and some are very unimportant. To know the difference is what we are given life to find out."
Anna F. Trevisan

take longer than we think. It also accounts for a wise anticipation of spur-of-the-moment demands on our time.

3. **"The Notorious Undocumented Commitment."** There are few things more dangerous than making a commitment without writing it down. If you honestly believe you can mentally file away that doctor's appointment or dinner reservation you just made, then you are giving yourself way too much credit. The human mind is not designed to hold onto small tidbits of information for days at a time. Write it down at the same time the commitment is made!

4. **"The Invasion of the Scrap Paper."** A note scratched on the back of an envelope is almost as devastating as having not written it down at all. The odds of you ever seeing the phone number again are next to nothing, but this is a lesson we all tend to re-learn a hundred times. Items should be documented only where they can be easily accessed later on. A logical "A to Z" tabbed file is an essential part of any planning system. Items need to be written down where they can be quickly found in your filing system.

5. **"Technological Quicksand."** Many new, exciting, and valuable electronic planning assistants arrive every three to four months, and they often bring the temptation to jump from your current format to this new gadget. Technology can certainly be a

big help in the planning process, but it can also make the process far too complicated. If time-saving technology takes more time to use than a pen and ink, then it is not saving you time. There is one key question to ask yourself when choosing time-saving technology:

Is it easy to access the information I need?

The Palm - platform Personal Digital Assistants are a great example of this problem. There is no way on a Palm to review a month-at-a-glance calendar on the PDA itself. If you are looking to find when a particular event takes place, this disadvantage can really slow you down. If the "month-at-a-glance" is important to you, you may find that the Palm platform may be inefficient for you.

The Final Piece in the Planning Puzzle

By now, you are feeling pretty efficient. If you have put half the stuff you have read so far into practice, you are already seeing some impressive results! As you are cruising toward those family goals, however, you need to finalize your plans for a filing system.

Filing is nothing but a fancy word for putting everything into an assigned place. It may or may not have anything to do with manila file folders. My friend Jonathan Falwell, Executive Pastor of Thomas Road Baptist Church, files almost everything electronically through a scanner that he keeps on his desk. He comes closer to maintaining a "paperless office" than anyone else I know. When he needs a document or piece of information, he can normally locate it fairly easily.

Here are several tips that have been useful to myself and others:

- **Alphabetize Everything.** The best filing systems I have ever seen are alphabetized. How you choose to alphabetize, however, is another question altogether. You generally have the choice of subject or name, and you simply want to choose the aspect you are most associated with. For example, if I am choosing whether to file my pest control company under its name or the simple category "Pest Control," I'll choose the category instead. I am less likely to remember the name of the person doing the work. However, inside the folder in my Pest Control file, I am going to write down the name of the person I am working with. This helps me to humanize the interactions in my week – reminding me in a small way that the people I come into contact with in everyday life are souls that Jesus wants to save.

- **Trash Your Excess Files!** The main reason people have such a difficult time locating the information they need is they have to wade through so much unnecessary data to find what they are looking for. Go through all the areas where your files are kept at least once a month and trash the stuff you do not need.

- **Maintain a Mobile System.** If you spend time away from your primary filing location, it is essential to maintain a mobile system as well. This allows for information to be filed immediately without getting lost in the shuffle. The best method I have seen is to combine the "A-Z" tabs in the address portion of most planners with the filing you need to accomplish. File paperwork here until it is needed if it will be in the next twenty-four hours, and transfer the paperwork to your main filing system if you do not need it for a long period of time.

- **"One File at a Time, Sweet Jesus. That's all I'm asking from You."** There should rarely be more than one file out of your system at any given moment. You can only work on one task at a time, and piling folders on your desk simply makes the job more difficult. Before you say, "It is a waste of my time to keep putting files away and getting other ones out," ask yourself how much time you waste digging for the information you need, and cleaning up piles on your workspace. When you were a child, your parents probably told you to put one toy away before playing with another. The same is true today, boys and girls!

- **Leave a Marker on the Trail.** Back in Cub Scouts, they taught us to mark our trail when hiking so that we could go back the way we came. Likewise, any filed information needs to be marked somewhere on your task list or calendar.

This reminds you there is information filed that needs to be acted on, and also points to it's current stored location.

The Power of Daily Planning (And the Danger of Its Absence)

When I was growing up, my dad ran the airport in Lockhart, Texas. I spent most of my adolescence around airplanes. We always had access to private planes, and would normally travel this way when we went on family trips. During long trips, it was not unusual for Dad to put me in the left seat and let me fly. I probably had over 100 hours logged before my 12th birthday.

Now, that may sound glamorous, but most of those trips were long and extremely boring. "Learning to fly" meant that I was relegated to watching a compass and adjusting the plane's direction with minute detail for hours at a time. My father would give me a compass heading to follow, and it was my job to point us in that direction. That, for the most part, was the essence of cross-country flying.

I remember one particular trip in which we were flying from Texas to Indiana to visit my grandmother. I was given the instructions on the direction to head soon after take-off, and left to do my duty. On this particular day, my dad was gaining confidence in my abilities I suppose, and was actually looking at something else there in the right seat. About two hours later, he looked up at the compass and noted that I was off two degrees from where he had asked me to travel. I responded that my direction might have been a couple of degrees off, but that we were certainly "close enough."

As you can imagine, moving two degrees off the destination point for two hours at close to 300 miles per hour can certainly make a tremendous difference in flight time! We lost considerable time on our journey, and Dad was less than impressed with my navigation abilities.

In the same way, if we are not making the daily adjustments and plans that sometimes seem so arduous, we have very little chance of actually reaching our long-term destination. Likewise, making specific plans daily and adjusting our tasks accordingly can save us valuable time later on. There is never a better time to begin adjusting your planning habits than today. The most important aspect of all in the planning process is simply to make a plan. Making even an inefficient plan every day is better than living by no plan at all.

Start your plans with family in mind, and build from there. Your plans will ultimately dictate the value of your time with the ones you love. Plan wisely, and you will have eternity to enjoy the results!

CHAPTER FOUR

TALK IS CHEAP ON THE HOME FRONT

THE POWER OF ACTION

Action is the final piece of the Home On Time puzzle. This is the piece that makes it go! **Without action, all of the response, direction, and planning is nothing but philosophy.** Nike™ was right all along. Sooner or later, you have to just do it.

This has always been a fascinating part of the Christian life to me, because God is the one who gives us strength to do anything, but He still allows us to play a part in the action. Even the most famous enabling verse of all shows the important balance between allowing God to work in our lives and taking action ourselves:

> "I can DO all things through Christ who strengthens me."– Philippians 4:13 (Emphasis Added)

Taking the first action step is often the most difficult part of any planning process. It is also the part that stalls success at home. Good intentions not acted upon have been the gateway to many destroyed homes and wayward children. **We cannot just *want* to do the right things, we actually have to take action!**

The Power of Action can be summed up this way:

By moving forward with wise action steps, I can attain the goals I have set for my family and my life. Action will be the ultimate test of success or failure in all of my pursuits.

I have been working in church ministry since my sophomore year in high school, and I have seen thousands of families in action. I have seen families that were headed for almost certain destruction and families that seemed almost to have a guarantee of success. When I really evaluate the essence of success or failure in these families, I find that their intentions of both kinds were often exactly the same. The common denominator of the successful families was simply this:

Successful families make an effort to do the small,

> "Laziness means more work in the long run."
> C.S. Lewis

meaningful things that other families only talk about doing.

More specifically...

Successful husbands put action to the words "servant leader." They faithfully lead the family in initiating spiritual disciplines in the home.

Successful wives offer loving support and respect to their husbands. They complement the marriage through their own strength and sensitivity.

Successful dads give time to kids, and participate in the activities that matter most to them.

Successful moms demonstrate their love through their "behind the scenes" sacrifices as well as through the words they speak.

Many Christians are uncomfortable talking about action, because they think it conflicts with the grace we receive in Christ. To presume that we can find success at anything through our own activities seems unspiritual! After all...

> "For by grace you have been saved through faith, and that not of yourselves; it is the gift of God, 9 not of works, lest anyone should boast." - Eph. 2:8,9

That is true. We can never earn the right to be good enough to have the relationship we enjoy with Jesus Christ. That comes from God's grace alone. **At the same**

time, God offers the principle that working toward positive goals has a long-term payoff. In fact, the very next verse in Scripture is often overlooked:

> "For we are His workmanship, created in Christ Jesus for good works, which God prepared beforehand that we should walk in them" - Eph. 2:10.

That is the idea behind Moses' concluding verses in Psalm 90. He has challenged us with a bleak picture of life and offered an alternate method of managing our time. Now he is asking God for help in taking appropriate action.

> "Return, O Lord! How long? And have compassion on Your servants. Oh, satisfy us early with Your mercy, that we may rejoice and be glad all our days!"

Moses is asking with a sense of desperation for God's renewed work. He longs for God to do great things in the presence of His people. In the same way, we need to consistently petition the Father to do great things in our midst. We seldom give God the credit He deserves for what He could do in our lives. Even more, we forget that God has promised to do great things through His people –people like you and me. **When we underestimate God's power, we ultimately underestimate our own power *through* Him!** Meaningful action begins with asking God for strength to get started.

Moses adds to this petition some specific parameters. He

asked that they be satisfied early. That certainly would make sense, because early morning was an important time of day for the Jews at the time this was written. Every morning when they arose, God had supplied them with manna from Heaven. This manna, their source of food for four decades in captivity, was scattered about on the desert floor. We do not know exactly what it was (apparently, they did not either. In Hebrew, the word manna simply means "what is it?"), but we can learn two significant lessons of how God provides for those He loves:

Learn to Master the Morning

Much has been written about finding your own peak hours of the day, and that can be helpful. Still, there is something universally productive about getting tasks done first thing in the morning. If nothing else, it gives you the day to enjoy the pleasures of accomplishment!

"The morning hour has gold in its hand."
Benjamin Franklin

- ■ The manna had to be gathered. God could have just as easily dropped manna at the doorsteps of their tents, or for that matter, on their kitchen tables. While He was working the miracle, why did He not just seal the deal? **God purposed that His people would participate in the miracle through actions of their own.** They had to work as part of the satisfaction that God was providing.

> To climb steep hills requires slow pace at first.
> Shakespeare

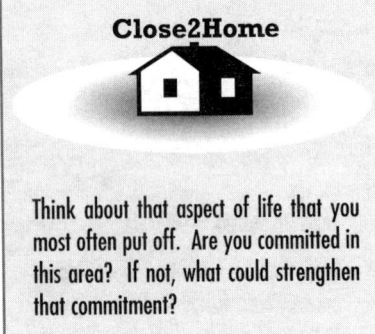

Close2Home

Think about that aspect of life that you most often put off. Are you committed in this area? If not, what could strengthen that commitment?

Many people believe it to be somehow more godly to sit back and do nothing, with the expectation that God will just drop success in their laps while they sit and wait. Very seldom has that ever happened. If we're not working toward our goals, we are missing out on the privilege of participation. There is tremendous joy in doing all we can and then watching God do more with our efforts than we ever could have on our own.

■ **Yesterday's manna meant nothing today.** The manna had to be gathered six days a week, and with the exception of Saturday, the food would be rotten after 24 hours.

Many of us have the tendency to rest on our past successes and expect to coast through current situations. Raising a family and cultivating a strong marriage are like most other things in life. **We are either moving forward or backwards. There is seldom room for idleness in the Christian life.** Moses' assertion at the end of this passage that they might rejoice and be glad all their days was no accidental figure of speech. Successful time management is a daily activity at its core.

"You may delay, but time will not."
Benjamin Franklin

> "Make us glad according to the days in which You have afflicted us, the years in which we have seen evil. Let Your work appear to Your servants, And Your glory to their children."

Moses asks that His people could see at least as many good days as the bad ones they had experienced. Even more, he is asking that the younger generation among them would be privileged to know even greater blessings than they experienced. That should be the essence of every parent's goal: to offer a spiritual heritage and legacy that exceeds our own. Some parents will have the privilege of initiating the very first spiritual legacy in the family's history. For others of us, we will be building on the Christian heritage that we received and are now passing down to our own children.

> "And let the beauty of the Lord our God be upon us, And establish the work of our hands for us; Yes, establish the work of our hands."

Moses ends the Psalm with a beautiful recipe for success – **the combination of *God's* help and *our* work.** He sums up all that he has observed, concluded, and petitioned from God with this very special request. He asks God to use us as His instruments in the world around us. **The idea is that we get to be a part of God's work – and that our work would have the significance of being the work of Almighty God!**

It certainly gives new meaning and significance to the closing request that the work of our hands would be established. As instruments of God, the actions we take have a tremendous significance. You now have the opportunity to act on God's behalf in the lives of those you love. You also have the responsibility to reflect God's work in your own actions.

If you want God to bless your spouse, then you should bless your spouse.

If you want God to give your children wisdom and strong decision-making skills, then you should take action in that area.

Saying we need to take action and actually taking it are two different things entirely. Here are two of the biggest roadblocks to action, and what you can do about it:

Phobias

Peladophobia: fear of baldness and bald people.

Aerophobia: fear of drafts.

Porphyrophobia: fear of the color purple.

Calyprophobia: fear of obscure meanings.

Thalassophobia: fear of being seated.

Stabisbasiphobia: fear of standing and walking.

Odontophobia: fear of teeth.

Graphophobia: fear of writing in public.

Phobophobia: fear of being afraid.

(From *Nothing to Fear*, by Fraser Kent, Doubleday & Company, 1977.)

Fear can be a debilitating force in your life if you allow it to stop your progress. Be brave — and move on!

Procrastination

Why do we put things off that we know need to get done? In an age of lightning fast computers and instant everything, we are still a culture of people who like to put things off. Procrastination can be a major stumbling block to success. We all have a tendency to save the most dreaded tasks for later - either out of mere avoidance or out of fear - but the danger in this is that later often gets lost with additional more desirable tasks.

Why do we procrastinate in the first place?

1. **Lack of Commitment and Desire.** If you are not committed to your plan, you will have no reason to complete your tasks. They will be put off. Every year, thousands of young men and women sign up for athletic teams in high schools across America. They subject themselves to organized physical torture and tremendous time sacrifice in order to be on a winning team. Of course, they are doing all this for free. So why do they keep coming back voluntarily? They are committed to the endeavor. Nothing in the world is more powerful than pure desire.

2. **Fear.** At times we choose to not move forward because we are simply afraid to fail. The perfectionist in you hesitates to do a job at all because she is afraid to do it the wrong way. The most important step of any task is getting started, and things are seldom perfect at the beginning of any

project. We learn as we go - but at least we are moving forward! Someone once said that "fear is interest paid on a debt you may not owe."

3. **Lack of Knowledge.** Sometimes our ignorance paralyzes us. I believe many moms and dads do not move forward with weekly family devotions in their homes because they simply do not know how to get started. They need more information. Perhaps you need to learn more about what you are trying to do before moving forward - but proceed with caution!

It is critical to remember the definition of time management when we are preparing for action: Time Management is doing the right things at the right time. When we act without doing the right things, our impulsiveness can end up doing more harm than good. King David spoke of this in Psalm 39:6:

"Surely every man walks about like a shadow; Surely they busy themselves in vain; He heaps up riches, And does not know who will gather them."

David should know about working in vain. The impulsive king that preceded him on the throne did everything in his power to destroy David. And David made his own impulsive mistakes, too.

God gives us more insight on this passage of Scripture in the verse that comes before it:

"Indeed, You have made my days as handbreadths, and my age is as nothing before You; Certainly every man at his best state is but vapor. Selah" Psalm 39:5

To be busy for the sake of being busy is the ultimate waste of time and eternity.

Searching out more information may just be another form of procrastination. Make sure you need more information on the task at hand. Once you have it, go and do.

Overcoming procrastination really has some very simple solutions. The key is that action has to be intentional. Remember that procrastination is nothing more than a habit, and habits can be changed!

A few habits to shoot for are:

- **Do unpleasant tasks first and get them over with.**

- **Take your least desirable tasks and break them into smaller tasks.**

- **Identify your least desirable tasks, and ask yourself if there is anyone that can assist you in the most unpleasant aspects of the work to be done, or identify an easier way to accomplish your goal.**

    If you are putting off exercise, for example, you might need to look at some new methods or equipment. But you still have to use them!

- **Give yourself a deadline and let others know**

"You can't build a reputation on what you are going to do."
Henry Ford

Close2Home

Treat Your Time Like the Treasure it Is!

Your time is valuable. Just as the time a CEO invests in his company will determine its outcome, so will the time you invest in your family make a difference in its success or failure.

Beware of opening lines like, "I just need a second of your time," or "Are you busy?" A time-robbing request or conversation may not be far behind — and your time is valuable!

what it is. If you meet that deadline, reward yourself!

■ We talked about fear being a cause of procrastination, but fear can be a powerful motivator as well. **Consider the consequences of NOT completing the task in a timely manner.** Will it mean a loss of income? A lack of healthy living? A loss of time with family? Fixing problems is usually a cheaper process if it is done as soon as possible.

Imagine how great it will feel to be done climbing that mountain of tasks in front of you. Start climbing now, and I guarantee you will enjoy the view from the top!

Time Wasters

Virginia Statesman John Randolph said more than two centuries ago that time is the most precious and most perishable of all our possessions.

> "It is wonderful how much may be done if we are always doing."
> Thomas Jefferson

We all know it, but how many of us have a level of frustration at what was accomplished through the course of a given day? Most people have the best intentions – especially with our top priorities – but find ourselves lacking at the end of the day.

So what can the average person do? Many of the priorities that are placed upon you each day can eat away at your own personal objectives. You may desire more time with the kids, but your boss at work desires more time on a project. At home, you may desire more sit-down dinners with the whole family, but kid's extracurricular activities rob you of that opportunity.

We all have areas of our lives where extensive amounts of time are thrown away with little benefit in return. No one is forcing you to waste this time, but it is taking large chunks out of your schedule. **Identifying and minimizing these key time wasters can literally add hours to your day!**

Close2Home

Caffeine is Not a Time Management Tool!

James Lane, Research Professor of Behavioral Medicine at Duke University, has found that people who drink caffeine and have stressful jobs experience more health problems than people who also have stressful jobs but do not consume caffeine.

(Taken from The Owner's Manual for The Brain, by Pierce J. Howard, Ph.D., Copyright 2001, Bard Press, Marietta, GA.)

"Our lives begin to end the day we become silent about things that matter."
Martin Luther King, Jr.

Here are some key time-wasters that affect many of us every day:

- **Telephone Interruptions.** At home or at work, when you have to stop an important task in order to answer the phone, you generally lose time with little payoff. There is power in answering machines and "caller ID." Except for emergencies, set aside a specific time later to return all of your calls.

- **Media Interruptions.** When you are working on a critical task, it is often more productive to turn off programs that are going to require your full attention. A great alternative is to videotape your favorite shows and view them on your schedule. Digital video recorders like TIVO™ have allowed families to plan out exactly what programs they will choose to enjoy, and helps reduce the hours spent channel-surfing. Continually ask yourself why a particular television program, magazine article, or radio show is worth your family's time. If it has no value, then you can probably find a better use for your time.

- **Clutter.** When your work is consistently interrupted by a frantic search for important items – even for just a few minutes – you are eating into a significant portion of your day. A few minutes taken to put things away can save valuable time later on. Even better, a weekend of effort spent giving your possessions a place to be put away might add years to your life!

Can Organizing my Home *Really* Add Years to My Life?

It certainly can. Two reasons:

- **Multi-Tasking.** This new-millennium buzzword may sound productive, but proceed with caution. Attempting too many things at once can drastically reduce the chances that those things will ever be completed. At the same time, finding tasks that can be done in a logical sequence can save time – like shopping at the mall where everything is in close proximity.

- **Rushing.** A hurried lifestyle not only leads to unnecessary stress. It can also lead to having to do things over. Waiting until the last minute and then kicking it into warp speed may be an adrenaline rush, but it rarely leads to quality work.

When it comes to family time in our busy lifestyles, every minute counts. Do not waste any more than you have to on time investments that give you nothing in return.

THE ADRENALINE CRUTCH – AN EMPTY CALL TO ACTION.

Here is the shortest quiz you will ever take in your life. It will help you diagnose whether this section is for you:
_____ "I work better under pressure."

> "That which we obtain too easily, we esteem too lightly."
> **Thomas Paine**

If you answered yes to that one question quiz, then I have news for you. You do not work better under pressure. **You might work harder under pressure, or faster under pressure, but studies have shown that you are certainly not *better* under pressure.**

Most of us became most acquainted with the power of the adrenaline rush while flirting with deadlines for school assignments. We waited until the last possible moment to complete an assignment before jumping on it with a mad rush of caffeine and the very real fear of a failing grade.

Working under a constant adrenaline rush minimizes our ability to think clearly, makes it difficult or impossible to do our best work, and can result in serious health problems over the long haul. Once again, there is absolutely no substitute for hard work over the long haul.

Self-Control

The Word of God is clear- we are called to be people who control ourselves. The word self-control simply means we do not need others to restrain us because we are able to show our own restraint – if we mess up, it is no one's fault but our own. Our inaction often comes down to a good old lack of discipline on our part.

I find it interesting that Peter speaks of self-control as a

> "A wise man will make more opportunities than he finds."
> Francis Bacon

weapon in defeating an attack by Satan. In I Peter 5:6-8, we are challenged to be self-controlled and alert in all we do. This reveals an important rule of success: self-control requires an understanding of personal weakness and a plan to prevent failures.

Fortunately, the Bible also gives some clear steps to self-control:

- **Prayer goes a long way toward self-discipline.** The best way to help ourselves is to acknowledge our helplessness to the One who can get us going!

- **Choose the *right* action.** If you choose no course of action, your life will be filled by the very behavior you are trying to avoid. If you are asking God for self-control over a bad habit, you might need to replace it with a new positive habit.

- **Ask for help.** If you are struggling with self-control in a certain area, ask someone you love and respect to encourage and pray for you.

Close2Home

Momentum May Be Overrated.

Momentum can be a great help once you have gotten started on a project, but watch out. If you get caught up in the excitement of activity, it is easy to branch out and take on unnecessary steps. Stay focused.

It is great to go "above and beyond" sometimes, but make sure you are still completing the original objective.

If your boss did not ask for anything but a simple report, don't waste your time designing a knockout report cover to go with it. You have better things to do.

S.T.E.P. Out and Get Started

If you are like me, sometimes there is as much dread as there is excitement when I'm told how to do something. Then the excuses are gone and there is nowhere to hide! Keep in mind that action will not be nearly as difficult when you have done the preparatory work found in this book. You may find that the action just comes more naturally now, but it will always take energy to get started with a task. And as long as it takes energy, there is a chance we will try to avoid it. Here are the critical, crowning STEPS to our planning process:

Schedule Your First Step. As we have already discussed, that first small step forward is the most critical one of all. It is the momentum builder that gets you to the next step, and the next, and the next... and you get the picture. I believe that 90% of failed projects do not succeed because they were never assigned this first step. I have gotten in the habit over the years of writing the word "HOW?" in large block letters after my speaking notes. When I am speaking, I try to remember that unless I give people the "how-to" of the challenge I'm issuing, I am setting them up for failure.

Every time you schedule something to do on your task list or calendar, be sure it includes a logical first step to action. You do not have to list every action step unless it really helps you plod through a boring task. This first

> "Those who are quick to promise are generally slow to perform. They promise mountains and perform molehills."
> — Charles Spurgeon

step will lead to the other ones very naturally. For example, you have been putting off the yard work for three weeks, and the flowerbed is starting to look like the Serengeti. Several trees need trimming, and the grass is out of control. Placing "yard work" on your calendar for this Saturday morning is an act of procrastination waiting to happen. However, placing "yard work: pull weeds first!" gives you a logical first step.

Close2Home

Are Routines a Burden or Reward?

Are your daily routines helping you meet your lifetime goals? Take a look at the things that you do almost automatically every day. With the knowledge you have gained about time management, decide whether they are saving effort over the long haul, or just wasting time on a regular basis.

Time Your Task. Give yourself a block of time in which only that task will receive your attention. It may seem illogical at first to be so stringent about a task, but you will find that it forces you to move forward. This is another reason why I recommend placing your priority tasks in time slots on your calendar rather than simply on a "to-do" list. Cleaning out closets may need to be done, but you will jump at the first alternate opportunity if given the chance. **You have to make a decision that, for an allotted period of time, that essential task gets all of your attention.** No phone calls, emails, television, or any other distractions that may pull you from your work.

Empty Your Excuse Bucket. This sounds a little too obvious, but hear me out on this one. Imagine that you hired a personal assistant to help you with your most challenging tasks – the ones you have been putting off for far too long. You are now paying this person big money to carry out these endeavors on your behalf. About a week after you outlined what needs to be done, you find that your assistant has made no progress whatsoever on your life's goals. Completely irritated, you demand to know the reason for this lazy behavior.

Now put yourself in the place of the do-nothing servant. After all, you are the best manager of your life you will ever find! What excuses would you give for not accomplishing these critical tasks? **Here is the key – by identifying up front what excuses could hinder progress to your goal, you will be able to dispel those excuses right from the start.** You basically can inoculate yourself from being sidetracked.

Press On. Once you have some momentum, the key is to keep moving. You do not have to be the best sprinter to win a marathon. You just have to keep going at a steady pace. Most people are surprised when they find out how little time over a consistent period a seemingly overwhelming task will take. Studies have shown, for example, that the average person, reading at a steady pace, could read the Bible cover-to-cover in about seventy-two hours. Over a year's time, that is less than twelve minutes a day! The Family Summit, spoken of in the Planning Section of this manual, is something that any family can do. Even if these family times are limited to a half an hour of prayer and discussion, that would equal 468 hours during your child's growing-up years! Do you think you would have a better opportunity to impart your values on your children with an extra 468 hours of time together?

The Hidden Power of Habits

Every day you live is a constant series of decisions. At its very core, time management is nothing more than a series of decisions about the events in which you choose to involve yourself. As a defense mechanism, our bodies have the ability to begin making decisions without any thought at all. These adjustments are called habits, and a habit is nothing more than a decision on "auto-pilot."

Exodus 12

When God instituted the Passover, He was commanding His people to commemorate what He was about to do – deliver them from the hands of slavery in Egypt. Why the symbolism? The clue is given in verses 26 and 27 of our passage:

"And it shall be, when your children say to you, 'What do you mean by this service?' that you shall say, 'It is the Passover sacrifice of the Lord, who passed over the houses of the children of Israel in Egypt when He struck the Egyptians and delivered our households.' So the people bowed their heads and worshiped." Exodus 12:26-27

When their children came and asked why they did this ceremony every year, the adult Jews had the most teachable moment possible to share what God had done!

Believe it or not, even small habits can have a tremendous impact on family life – primarily because bad habits can

> "God nowhere tells us to give up things for the sake of giving them up. He tells us to give them up for the sake of the only thing worth having - life with Himself."
> Oswald Chambers

waste the family's most precious commodity – time. And if it is argued that money is the family's second most precious commodity, then bad habits can place that in jeopardy too.

Big or small, bad habits are a part of the family landscape. They may be as simple as saying "you know" every few words, drinking coffee all day, biting your fingernails, or popping your knuckles. On the other hand, they may be as complicated as smoking or bad language. And let's not forget overspending and overeating – those two great American icons!

When we realize that these habits cost us something in the long run, whether it is money, wasted time, or injured relationships, it should motivate us to do something about them.

Still, wanting to kick a habit and actually doing so are two different things entirely. According to the USA Today (July 26, 2002), seven in ten adult smokers in the United States say they want to quit, but most find themselves helpless to do so.

What can you do to overcome these aspects of life that are so ingrained into our every day activities? Here are seven key steps to breaking bad habits:

1) First, **you have to be convinced you want to**

> "You got to be very careful if you don't know where you're going, because you might not get there."
>
> Yogi Berra

break bad habits – the benefits must be obvious and motivation must be there.

2) Next, i**dentify what they are.** Write down your bad habits. Being aware of a bad habit helps you stop doing it.

3) Third, **think of an alternative for each bad habit** and write it down. You will have an instant replacement activity as soon as the temptation occurs rather than trying to think in the heat of the moment.

4) Fourth step - once you have made the list, **choose one bad habit to work on first.** Take it gradually, working on one habit at a time.

5) **Declare your intentions** to break a particular habit publicly – to friends, family, and co-workers. Once it is public knowledge, it will be harder to take back and may provide the motivation to keep trying.

6) Next, **find a friend or loved one who is trying to break the same habit.** This will provide both motivation and someone to call when you are tempted to cheat.

7) And finally, **reward yourself** with something meaningful to you when you have replaced your bad habit – a new outfit or a weekend getaway, for example.

We automatically think of habits in the negative sense of the word, but **habits can be a greater asset than you might imagine!** Anything done consistently over a period of time will automatically fit into this category, and positive habits are no exception.

Remember, breaking bad habits takes time and discipline. Starting good habits does too. As you begin taking action with your new planning goals, choose one or two small habits you can develop over the next forty days. If you can consistently do anything for a forty-day period, you will find you are not far off from a life-long habit.

The Ancient Power of Forty Days

In the fall of 2000, something very special happened at Thomas Road Baptist Church, the church where I was serving as Family Pastor at the time. As a church family, we embarked on a forty-day journey together between Thanksgiving and Christmas. This short period of time and the simple forty-days' journey that accompanied it became the catalyst for some very exciting transformations in the families of our church. Stories of couples who began praying together, family traditions that were rekindled, and homes that were brought back under control were just a few of the examples of what God did in our midst during this special journey.

Forty Days with the Family was meant to be a small and simple "jump start" for families – a place that, if not life-changing, would challenge men and women of God to consider the eternal impact of their family routines. The extraordinary results we received, I believe, are based not on any particularly profound content. The original Forty Days guides were mostly personal stories from my own experiences, successes, and failures. Instead, I strongly believe now that there is something very special about doing something for forty days.

I believe there are some very practical reasons that a forty-day experience is significant:

1. **It creates an attainable goal.** Almost anyone can find success in a small task for forty days. With a little determination, the most distracted among us can make it that far.

2. **It is long enough to leave an impression.** Researchers have touted 21 days as the magic number by which new habits can be formed. If that is true, then surely doubling that time period is long enough to leave an impression that lasts a lifetime. Forty days is often long enough that participants have to make some sacrifices for success to happen. It is long enough for momentum to get a running start.

3. **We see evidence of this in Scripture several times.** Perhaps the most famous example, Noah found himself in forty days of rain that began a five-month flood – encased in a floating ark of salvation with his family (Genesis 6-11). Moses spent forty days on Mount Sinai with God in the 24th chapter of Exodus. Jesus fasted for forty days in

the wilderness before beginning his public ministry (Matthew 4:1-2). Following the resurrection of Christ, the disciples had the privilege of spending forty precious days learning about the truths of the Kingdom (Acts 1:3).

When it comes down to the nitty-gritty of actually doing a task for forty days, only your perception of its importance will keep you going. No magic number is going to change your habits. You have to make the time commitment to make it happen. You may have to remove some items from your schedule for this short period of time in order to come up with ten to fifteen minutes a day that will be necessary.

This small investment has the potential to reap dividends that you never thought possible! A fantastic first step to take after completing this workbook would be to utilize the bonus workbook section titled, *The First Forty Days*. Just ten minutes a day can help you develop an ongoing habit you will not regret.

The Forgotten Power of Family Traditions

When you were a child, was there something special that your family did every year without fail? Many of us can remember special traditions during the holidays that still make us smile.

When I speak on family traditions, I often ask for examples from the audience. Any time I ask in Virginia, I never fail to have people share that every Christmas morning their family shared oyster stew together. With apologies for anyone who might be touched by the proud Old-Dominion ritual, I cannot qualify that as a tradition. A really gross practice maybe – or a neat way to give everyone bad breath at the very beginning of the day perhaps – but not exactly what I had in mind!

Traditions have always been a powerful and significant part of Jewish culture. Yet sometimes traditions have often been thought of in a negative connotation – outdated symbols that have no meaning. At their origins, the Hebrew traditions served a very important purpose. They reminded God's people of His timeless principles. Behind every symbol, there was substance of eternal significance!

Many of us have thrown the concept of family traditions out the windows of our homes. We may have things we do every week, every month, or every year, but they may not contain the critical components that make traditions so valuable. Without these important elements, the things we do in our homes are not traditions – they are just family habits.

Traditions have three key components:

1. **They are intentional.** "Every Friday morning we have breakfast together as a family." Traditions do not happen by accident.

2. **They are things that we look forward to.** "We all pitch in to make a delicious and fun breakfast."

3. **There is a higher purpose than the activity itself.** "More than just a meal, this has helped us maintain a strong sense of identity as a family and allowed us to keep track of everything that is happening outside the home."

Traditions do not have to be as complicated as you might imagine. **The simple act of doing something special on a regular basis will add a level of expectation, anticipation, and stability to your family life.** That is the essence of the planning process, and the foundation of my passion for the home itself. By establishing this consistency at home, we build a life structure that maintains and even cultivates a great marriage, and one that gives kids every chance to grow in character during the short time they are entrusted to our hands.

The Stuff That Really Matters

To illustrate how simple – but meaningful – these family traditions can be, I will share one of my own. Every night before my two daughters go to sleep, I get the privilege of tucking them in bed. We pray together, sometimes spend some time memorizing Scripture, and then do our hugs and kisses. Then comes the tradition.

Every night without fail, both of my girls will look at me with sleepy eyes and say, "Daddy, give me something to dream about." Then I share some wild, far-fetched plot with them to set the stage for an exciting dream adventure. Some might wonder what real purpose such a tradition has, or what on earth that tradition has to do with time management. To me, the answer to this is the best way to conclude our study together.

By giving my girls something to dream about every night for as long as they will let me, I am afforded the chance to share with them again and again that they can do anything they put their minds to. I want them to leave our home someday with the strong sense of confidence and imagination that come from thousands of big dreams.

Most of all, I will always cherish the moments I get to share life with the two most important little girls in my universe. I pray daily that the legacy I leave them during these special times will last long after I am gone.

Perhaps a hundred years from now, my great-grandson will lean over the bed of my great-great granddaughter, taking the time to give her something to dream about.

That is what *I* dream about. God bless you, and dream big!

You're Not Done Yet!

Before closing the book, don't forget to complete the Family Time Inventory and get started with the bonus workbook titled, *The First Forty Days*. This section is full of ready-to-use applications that will get you moving in the right direction! At the conclusion of this forty-day period, you will want to complete the "Post-Book" edition of the Balanced Life Inventory.

CHAPTER FIVE

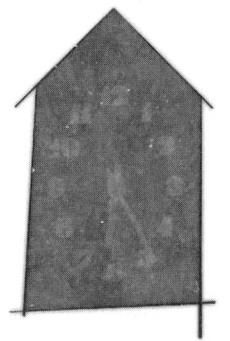

THE GREATEST NEWS IN THE ENTIRE BOOK

There is one decision in life that is more critical than any other by far – one element that will literally make all the difference in the world when you die. Would an *honest* obituary of you be able to make the following claim, "He knew without a doubt that he would be spending eternity in heaven"? If there is any doubt at all as to whether this is true for you, the most critical step you can take at this point is outlined in the bonus section on the following page. Please take a few minutes to read this life-changing information before going any further!

The Decision that Lasts an Eternity...

Talking about Heaven and Hell is at times an uncomfortable experience – because many are unsure of where they fit in this mystery. But we don't have to be confused. The Bible has outlined exactly how we can understand this important subject.

1. At the very foundation of the world, God created mankind in His own image to have fellowship with Him. Even today, men and women are created and ultimately fulfilled in this very special relationship. Many people who have come to know God have later commented on how that bond filled a void they had felt all of their lives but they had never been able to fill.

2. Here's the bad news – God is perfect, and we are not! The Bible says that, *"All have sinned and fall short of the glory of God." (Romans 3:23),* and also that *"...The wages of sin is death..." (Romans 6:23).* If God is perfect, and we are all imperfect, then the Bible is saying that we must be separated from God.

3. In fact, it would be impossible for God to allow sin into Heaven. So how can sinful man reconcile this problem so that we can have the relationship we were created to have?

4. God solved that problem for us. He sent His only Son, Jesus Christ, to earth. Jesus was born of the virgin Mary, and lived a life completely without sin. And yet, this one single person in all of history who qualified for the perfection necessary to escape penalty, chose to die on a cross as payment for all of OUR sins!

5. It is up to you whether you choose to receive this free gift. Eternal life and forgiveness is offered through the sacrifice of Jesus Christ. In order to receive this gift, you must trust Him and confess that you want to receive it. The Bible says, *"That if you confess with your mouth that Jesus is Lord, and believe in your heart that God raised Him from the dead, you shall be saved."* (Romans 10:9)

6. There is nothing that you can ever do in order to earn the free gift of eternal life. It is no accident that God has placed you here today in front of this life-changing news. Are you willing to pray right now, and begin this new life in Christ? Your own prayer from your heart might sound something like this:

Lord Jesus, I know that I am a sinner. I confess my sins, and realize that I can never be good enough on my own to get to heaven. Thank you for dying on the cross for my sins. I accept your free gift of forgiveness, and I am beginning a brand new life today – one without the guilt of all the blame you've taken away. Thank you for saving me, Lord. Amen.

If you made this wonderful choice today, we can help you get started right in this brand new journey. Home on Time has some free resources available just for you at www.homeontime.com. You should also consider letting a Christian friend or pastor know of your decision, so that they can rejoice with you and help you grow spiritually in this new relationship.

Family Time Inventory - **Response**

My Sphere of Influence You and your family first, then close co-workers and friends.	How I Want to Influence Give a brief statement on how your role should make a difference in his or her life.	Outside Forces that Affect My Influence These immovable obstacles will need to be identified and adjusted for in your plan.	Upcoming Major Milestones Anticipated events in the future that will have a major impact on this person. How can this become an opportunity for influence?
You			
Spouse			
Child			
Family, Co-Workers, and Friends			

Family Time Inventory - Direction

	Lifetime Goals	Long-Term Goals	Short-Term Goals
The Goal Quadrant - These four areas encompass a balanced effort at success in life.	Write down the long-range outcome you hope to accomplish in this area. You might even write it in the third person / past-tense: "She made sure all of her children knew that they were loved and accepted."	Write down the objectives that will help you move closer to your life-time goals over the next five - ten years. They may be tied to a specific date, like the high-school graduation of a child.	Identify goals that can be accomplished in six months to a year that will move you closer to attaining your long-term goals.
Mind Goals - I have a responsibility to sharpen my mind, and to grow in wisdom throughout life.			
Body Goals - I will strive to strengthen my body and keep it healthy. The care and effort I put forth physically is a reflection of my spiritual discipline.			
God Goals - As with any other relationship, growth comes through time together and deeper knowledge.			
People Goals: Family - I will place a high priority in ensuring the spiritual well-being of my home through Safety and Legacy.			
People Goals: Church - God calls me to make an impact through serving others. I will commit to invest time and effort as a part of my local church.			
People Goals: Community - I will be a positive voice to those around me, serving as salt and light to my community.			

Family Time Inventory - Planning and Action

Key Decisions	Plan of Attack Describe some ways you can make this work best in your life. Next to "Focus Time," should be something like, "Purchase a 'One-Year Bible' and combine this with a new Bible study habit."	Time and Location Write down the specifics of HOW you hope to accomplish this plan: "I will find one place to serve in my church at least once a week in the children's department."	Action Steps What immediate and ongoing actions need to happen to prepare for this new plan? What needs to be removed from your schedule to make room for this?
Family Summit: Customize a plan for instituting this weekly ritual in your home.			
Focus Time: Establish a daily routine of prayer, devotion, evaluation, and planning.			
Habits and Routines: First, I must remove negative habits from my life. At the same time, I need to create new habits so essential tasks happen automatically.			
Family Traditions: I will create or renew special times for my family that will underscore our core values.			
Forty Days Plan: I will capitalize on the next forty days to begin developing new, positive habits in my life.			

Planning Tools: Write down the tools that you plan to use for your calendar, task list, and filing system. Remember - simplicity and ease of use are the keys to success!

SPECIAL BONUS SECTION: THE FIRST FORTY DAYS

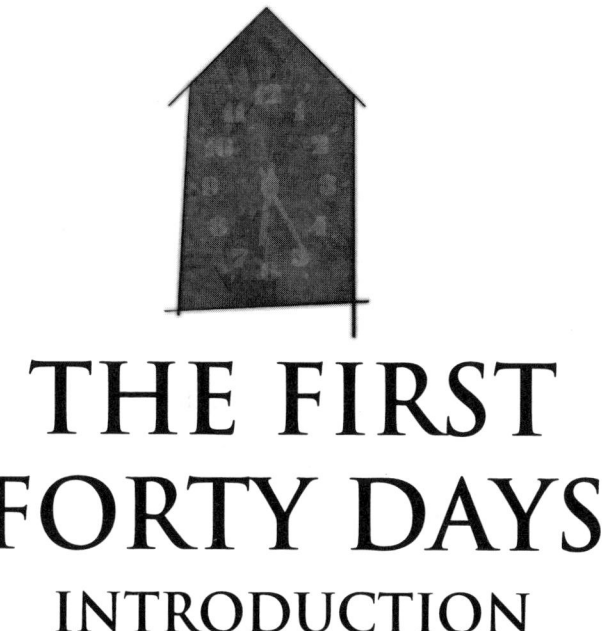

THE FIRST FORTY DAYS
INTRODUCTION

When it comes down to the nitty-gritty of actually DOING this forty-day experiment, only your perception of its importance will keep you going. No magic number is going to change your habits. You have to make a choice to commit this time. You may need to remove some items from your schedule for this short period of time in order to come up with the ten to fifteen minutes a day that you will need. Considering that this fifteen-minute commitment can add years to your life, it is certainly worth the sacrifice!

The First Forty Days will feature a "Secrets to Success" article each week to get you going, and a "Jump-Start Checklist" to help you with practical action steps. These do not have a specific day assigned to them, but simply should be completed through the week as you find time. The key element is a simple daily checklist, where you will hold yourself accountable for the activities you have made a commitment to complete. You will notice each week that there is a fill-in-the-blank journal to document your personal progress. You will choose your own Scripture passage to memorize every seven days as well. Because of this weekly breakdown, it is strongly recommended that you begin your journey on a Sunday. This allows for a special reflection and planning time each Sunday to correspond with worship attendance.

I can promise you one thing of which we can both can be very sure. There is nothing in your life so critical that it should usurp your walk with God and the strength of your family. In light of eternity, I can think of nothing even close to these priorities in the Kingdom. May God bless your faithfulness as you commit to this very special journey.

My Goal Quadrant for the Next Forty Days:

Body Goals:

- Beginner's Suggestion: Half hour of exercise for three days per week.

- Advanced Suggestion: Three days per week of aerobic exercise, and three days per week of resistance training.

- Minimum Goal: Commitment to a healthy diet.

Mind Goals:

- Beginner's Suggestion: Read two books during the forty days that will increase essential knowledge.

- Advanced Suggestion: Read a knowledge-building book each week.

- Minimum Goal: Begin taking notes during Bible studies, lectures, and sermons. Write a personal application.

God Goals:

- Beginner's Suggestion: Ten minutes per day of prayer and Bible study.

- Advanced Suggestion: Incorporate one hour of prayer and Bible study into your daily routine. Use part of this time for silence and listening to God.

- Minimum Goal: Memorize John 15 during the six-week period.

People Goals:

- Beginner's Suggestion: Invite a neighbor over whom you do not know and share the joy of your family.

- Advanced Suggestion: Find a new place of service in your church where you can participate in helping others.

- Minimum Goal: Resolve to be an encourager to at least one person per day.

Week One: Getting Started Right

Steps to Success: Identifying Yes's and No's

I trust that you have some major goals in mind for the coming forty days. Dreaming makes life exciting, and I for one like to dream BIG. Part of reaching our dreams, however, is learning to remove distractions from our lives. And removing distractions involves learning the word, "No." Many of us have a difficult time declining commitments, even if they take us away from the direction we feel we should be going.

In the computer world, programmers have made it clear that even the most sophisticated PC's recognize only two things - 1's and 0's - and all computer languages can be reduced to long strings of these two digits. Likewise, our lives can be reduced to our "yes's and no's." Which response we choose will have a dramatic effect on the legacy we leave. Saying yes to extra hours at work in order to get a promotion means saying no to hours at home that mean the world to your children. Saying yes to extracurricular activities means saying no to other priorities.

Over these next six weeks, you will see one major theme during our journey together: *Removing the Clutter from Life*. Clutter comes in all shapes and sizes. Clutter can be more than the paperwork that is covering your desk. Clutter may be the unnecessary appointments on your calendar. Be sure that you are saying "yes" to the things that matter most in life!

Choose today to begin identifying the things that are most precious to you in life. By identifying those things that are the most valuable, you'll begin to notice the items that are cluttering your life and keeping you from the fulfillment you want to enjoy.

> "Therefore we also, since we are surrounded by so great a cloud of witnesses, let us lay aside every weight, and the sin which so easily ensnares us, and let us run with endurance the race that is set before us" (Hebrews 12:1).

Jump-Start Checklist: Nine Steps to Purchasing the Perfect Planner

1. There is no one perfect planner. Select one that moves like you do – get a convenient size for your lifestyle, handwriting, personality, etc. The number-one priority is to have a planner that you will be comfortable carrying with you at all times.

2. Select a calendar with the level of detail that reflects the specifics of your life. If you require a large number of daily appointments in order to be successful, you may prefer a "page-per-day" format. If your success is dictated by the ability to respond successfully, then a "page-per-week" may prevent you from overscheduling.

3. If your thinking flows well when you are typing or inputting information, and you are comfortable working from a computer screen, a digital planner may be right for you. The downside of a digital assistant is the inability to easily add loose paper documents that are acquired as you move through the day.

4. If you do collect a number of critical documents during a given day, then paper planners may be your best choice.

A simple filing system will allow you to store the document instantly so it is ready when you need it.

5. While it may seem convenient to carry, selecting a planner that is too small in size may end up being counterproductive.

6. Stay away from using multiple calendars – even if it seems more convenient in the short term. Trying to coordinate desk calendars, wall calendars, computer calendars, and personal planners almost assures the loss of essential data. Stick to one system and keep it with you at all times.

7. Once you have selected your planner, decide immediately where you plan to store each piece of information until you need it. Keep it simple, and do not stray from your system of management. Using your "A to Z" pages (often included in the address section) to file away documents until they are needed can be a great solution. For example, put critical travel information for an upcoming trip behind the "T" tab in your planner.

8. Don't just use your planner to write down future plans, but also to record events as they happen. Documenting phone calls, appointments, tasks that weren't planned for, expenses and events will help you reference them in the future.

9. On your appointments list, be sure to document the location of any related items that will be essential to completing the objective.

Week One Checklist:	S	M	T	W	Th	F	S
God Goals							
Scripture Memory Work	❏	❏	❏	❏	❏	❏	❏
Daily Focus (Prayer and Study) Time	❏	❏	❏	❏	❏	❏	❏
Personal Goals_____	❏	❏	❏	❏	❏	❏	❏
People Goals							
Encourage One Person	❏	❏	❏	❏	❏	❏	❏
Personal Goals_____	❏	❏	❏	❏	❏	❏	❏
Mind Goals							
Gained Wisdom through Reading, Audio Message, etc.	❏	❏	❏	❏	❏	❏	❏
Personal Goals_____	❏	❏	❏	❏	❏	❏	❏
Body Goals							
Healthy Eating Habits	❏	❏	❏	❏	❏	❏	❏
Personal Goals_____	❏	❏	❏	❏	❏	❏	❏

Week One Notes and Observations:

_____
_____
_____
_____
_____
_____
_____
_____
_____
_____
_____

Week Two: Organizing My Life

Steps to Success: Stopping the Clutter Where it Starts

Clutter – we all have it. And even those of us who try and rid our homes of clutter find ourselves having to clear it out over and over again. For many of us, ridding our homes of unnecessary items is not simply a one-time-never-repeated event. Because of this, the first step in clearing our homes of clutter is to find out just WHY we have all this stuff in the first place!

Once you have identified the sources, you'll be on your way to ridding your life of the clutter that slows you down.

Clutter comes into your life in three ways:

You take it in. We bring things with us from Mom and Dad's house when we first move out on our own. We get free calendars from salesmen and free cologne samples from the nice people at the department store. We collect free brochures on potential vacation spots. This is the kind of stuff we choose to bring into our homes, but who can blame us – it's free, right?

It's given to you. These are items such as birthday, anniversary, and holiday gifts. People may also give us gifts when we get married and move into our first home. Then we receive items to pass along through the family, like Grandmother's china or Uncle Joe's old golf clubs. This is often complicated by the fact that when these family items are presented to us, we often can't turn them down without hurting someone's feelings. So again, we take them into our homes and try to find a place for them. To make matters even more complicated, sometimes these gifts are inherited, and you feel guilty about letting it go. Family members pass on and their stuff finds it's way into our possessions. You may receive hand crocheted linens that are so old, they cannot be used any longer. Or you may find you are the owner of an old guitar that no longer works. Whatever it is, it's yours now and again you must find a place for it.

You buy it. Now we're getting to the heart of the matter! Some of the stuff we buy is necessary and we truly do need it. But much of what we buy is impulsive and useless. You may silently ask yourself later – "What was I thinking when I bought that combination fruit dryer/rice steamer?" – but not wanting to admit a shopping mistake, we keep all that stuff and try to find places for it, too!

Here's the key – once you have identified where clutter is leaking into your life, you have to make the necessary changes to improve results. Remember that everything you own owns your time in some way, and it is your responsibility to monitor the amount of clutter that flows into your life.

When it comes to clutter, we are generally one of 5 personalities types.

The Hoarder – this person feels they will never have all the resources they need if they let go of any possessions. They hang onto clutter because it might come in handy someday!

The Deferrer – this person never gets around to clearing any clutter because they believe they will have more time and energy tomorrow. This personality is a procrastinator and believes in thinking about it tomorrow.

The Rebel – this is someone who was forced to pick up as a child and refuses to now as an adult. They will not pick up dirty laundry or dishes because Mom's not here and they don't have to!

The Perfectionist – lives in an all-or-nothing world. They have a fear of doing a less than perfect job so unless they have 110% to devote to clearing out the clutter, they'll just let it slide.

The Sentimentalist – is a nice way of saying a packrat! This person never met a memento they didn't like – and keep! The problem is the items worth really hanging onto, like wedding pictures usually end up lost in a flood of clutter.

Now we have a reason for why we hang onto stuff but that shouldn't give us an excuse for not clearing out the mess!

Ted W. Engstrom said that, "Anything that is wasted effort represents wasted time. The best management of our time thus becomes linked inseparably with the best utilization of our efforts."

Don't waste more effort than necessary shuffling around the clutter in your life. Identify you clutter quotient, and take action this week.

Jump-Start Checklist:
Twelve Steps Toward Organization

1. The first step of strong organization at home is setting up a central command center from which all documents, calendars, and correspondence starts and stops. This is your household's information hub – an actual spot for

handling all the paper and information related to daily living.

2. Keep some basic supplies in your command center so that you are not running all over the house when you get ready to pay bills or take care of correspondence. Some items to include in your supply drawer or basket are pens, paper clips, scissors, glue sticks, post-it notes, envelopes, a supply of greeting cards, and stamps.

3. Keeping a Master List at the command center is also a good idea. A Master List is kind of like a to-do list, except that it has no deadlines or boundaries. This is the where you dump everything that comes up during the day. These include tasks that you'd like to do or feel you need to do that suddenly pop into your head. The main thing is to get them all down in one place. When you are planning your daily to-do list, you can consult this Master List.

4. Maintain a single **action pile** for items that require you to do something **simple**. It may be pay a bill, read it, or write it down. For example, a birthday party invitation arrives in the mail. Open the card, write the information down in your calendar and throw out the invitation.

5. For documents that will require longer attention, file them in an appropriate location and reference the document in your planner for future attention.

6. Set up a system for filing and storage of those files. Keep it as simple as possible. For most people, alphabetizing by topic makes the most sense.

7. Label everything clearly.

8. Be sure that your filing system is easy to use not just for you, but for others who need to access your information.

9. Maintain convenient access to a **giveaway pile**. This is made up of items that might be of interest to someone else, such as a friend or family member. For example, you may receive a packet of coupons for diapers and no longer have a baby in the home. This would be a good item to pass along to someone you know who does have a baby.

10. The most important organizational tool of all is a conveniently located trash can. Junk mail definitely belongs here– don't even bother to open it up. It's a good idea to open your mail over the trash so you can immediately toss out any unnecessary items. It goes from mailbox to trashcan and never has to touch your desktop or counter.

11. A word of caution about reading material: Keep up with all reading material on a daily basis. If you can't, then you have too much. An easy way to rid your home of excess paperwork is not to subscribe to magazines and newspapers in which no one has the time or interest to actually read! Be honest with yourself. If you're probably never going to read it, it doesn't belong in the action pile.

12. Never walk away from your workspace with loose papers laying out and unaccounted for. Everything should be in place so that the next visit is an efficient one, and paperwork is not lost in the meantime.

Week Two Checklist:	S	M	T	W	Th	F	S
God Goals							
Scripture Memory Work	❏	❏	❏	❏	❏	❏	❏
Daily Focus (Prayer and Study) Time	❏	❏	❏	❏	❏	❏	❏
Personal Goals_____	❏	❏	❏	❏	❏	❏	❏
People Goals							
Encourage One Person	❏	❏	❏	❏	❏	❏	❏
Personal Goals_____	❏	❏	❏	❏	❏	❏	❏
Mind Goals							
Gained Wisdom through Reading, Audio Message, etc.	❏	❏	❏	❏	❏	❏	❏
Personal Goals_____	❏	❏	❏	❏	❏	❏	❏
Body Goals							
Healthy Eating Habits	❏	❏	❏	❏	❏	❏	❏
Personal Goals_____	❏	❏	❏	❏	❏	❏	❏

Week One Notes and Observations:

_____
_____
_____
_____
_____
_____
_____
_____
_____
_____
_____
_____

Week Three: Staying Focused

Foundations of Focus

My camera, like most today, has a feature called "auto-focus." I don't have to adjust the lens by hand, because the electronics can automatically detect distance, size, and all of the other things that photographers used to do by hand. Unfortunately, sometimes the camera focuses on the wrong object, such as a branch closer to the camera, and the image I am aiming at becomes blurry and unclear. In order to focus properly – even with the "auto-focus" engaged – I must be sure that these distracting objects are out of view.

When we talk about a desire to live more focused lives, that means we want to bring our desired goals into clear view with logical steps that will get us there, and without any obstacles in the way to distract us. Listed below are two of the most fundamental elements of a focused lifestyle:

Rest and Worship.

We live in a weary world. Most people live life filled with exhaustion, looking to each new day with frustration and dread. This is hardly what God had in mind for us!

In the Old Testament, God commanded His people to "remember the Sabbath and keep it holy." The Sabbath was a day set aside for both rest and worship. From the very beginning, God meant for the two to go together. When we worship God, we will find the rest that we long for. When we get appropriate rest, we will be better worshippers!

Jesus said, "Come unto me all you who are weary..."

(Matthew 11:28) When you are weary and tired, the solution is first to go to Jesus. The REST does not come through lack of work, but from being with the Lord.

The greatest vacation in the world can't give us the rest we need unless that rest is combined with worship.

A Family Charter.

On July 4, 1776, the founders of America sat down and penned perhaps the greatest charter in the history of mankind – the Declaration of Independence. This incredible document set forth the foundational vision for the freedom that we enjoy today. These men not only wrote down what they planned to do. They penned the reasons for their beliefs and the core convictions that were to be the bedrock for generations to come.

The principle still stands: when you want to pass something on to future generations, it must be written down in a way that can never be disputed. You must nail down what you believe and your top priorities as a family.

Write down the essential elements of your vision today, and review them often. When we establish our life focus through a family charter, built on high Biblical standards, and follow through on that charter with the rest and worship that God commands, we are ready to move forward with confidence.

Jump-Start Checklist: Ten Colossal Steps to Creating a Calendar

1. Take a week-long inventory of where your time goes. Identify time wasters, areas that could be condensed into less time, and areas that are the most important to you and your goals.

2. Identify areas in your day in which you seem to be the most effective. Try and place your most critical tasks into this time slot.

3. Rather than documenting every planned activity, create time blocks on your calendar for each general category. For example, block off a time period each day at the same time for checking email, returning phone calls, writing letters, and filing documents.

4. Build daily rituals into your calendar to increase predictability: "Every weekday morning at 6:30, I will block off a half-hour for focus time."

5. After you place your daily rituals on the calendar, place your weekly traditions there: "Every Friday morning, we will eat breakfast together as a family."

6. Anticipate how long each calendar event will last, and then double that time slot. Actions often take longer than you think they will, and that carries over to the next activity. Overloading the calendar only leads to frustration.

7. Block off your calendar in thirty-minute increments rather than fifteen-minute ones. This will help prevent over-scheduling.

8. Some flexible tasks don't need to be represented on your calendar at all. If they need to be done, but not necessarily by a specified time, then they should be placed on your task list instead.

9. Make appointments for anything that has to be done today. Do not fall in the trap of just leaving it on your task list with three stars by it. Block off the time to ensure it gets done.

10. Depending on your station in life, you will need to block off certain amounts of "response time" in your schedule. If much of your day is involved in crisis management – activities that cannot be anticipated exactly but for which you must be available – then you need to plan for this time in your calendar.

Week Three Checklist:	S	M	T	W	Th	F	S
God Goals							
Scripture Memory Work	❏	❏	❏	❏	❏	❏	❏
Daily Focus (Prayer and Study) Time	❏	❏	❏	❏	❏	❏	❏
Personal Goals_____	❏	❏	❏	❏	❏	❏	❏
People Goals							
Encourage One Person	❏	❏	❏	❏	❏	❏	❏
Personal Goals_____	❏	❏	❏	❏	❏	❏	❏
Mind Goals							
Gained Wisdom through Reading, Audio Message, etc.	❏	❏	❏	❏	❏	❏	❏
Personal Goals_____	❏	❏	❏	❏	❏	❏	❏
Body Goals							
Healthy Eating Habits	❏	❏	❏	❏	❏	❏	❏
Personal Goals_____	❏	❏	❏	❏	❏	❏	❏

Week One Notes and Observations:

_____
_____
_____
_____
_____
_____
_____
_____
_____
_____

Week Four: Becoming Available to Your Family

Secrets to Success: Making the Most of Mealtimes

In today's fast-paced world, what difference could it possibly make whether your family eats at the same time? Studies show that it actually makes a tremendous difference!

According to a study at the American Psychological Association's 105th Annual Convention, adjusted teens (adjusted meaning they are less likely to do drugs, less likely to be depressed, more motivated at school, and have better peer relationships) eat with their families an average of 5 days a week.

A Reader's Digest article by Rachel Wildavsky titled *What's Behind Success in School?* found that kids who regularly shared mealtimes with their families tested better than those who did not.

Exactly what aspect of the event makes it so effective is not clear, but it does appear that family mealtimes play an important role in helping families deal with the pressures of adolescence. Most likely it is the by-products of the event – and not the dining itself – that make such a difference: togetherness, communication, understanding, teaching, and encouragement.

Even for families who have a strong desire to make it happen, eating together is still easier said than done. Here are three important points to keep in mind.

1. Be Realistic.
If we are going to make lasting mealtime traditions, we have to set some realistic parameters. If you decide to eat together every night from now on and have never been able to pull

it off before, you will probably not last long.

Set a goal of three to five times a week if you are not in the habit at all. Give yourself every chance for success by setting the tone with a mealtime blessing and soft music in the background. Set the stage for pleasant conversation with some ground rules against bickering and complaining – with parents setting the example. Remove as many distractions as possible. For example, let the answering machine get the phone. Eliminating distractions lets your family know that this time together takes precedence.

2. Be Creative.
Part of being realistic is finding creative solutions to impossible problems.

If one spouse works late and does not always make it home before the family has eaten, consider a special dessert time with the kids. This will take less time than a full meal, the kids will not be cranky and starving from having to wait for dinner, and you can eat dessert after kids are completely ready for bed.

If you have older children who are heavily involved in outside activities, you might plan for a family mealtime away from home as well. A bucket of chicken in the gym parking lot together is still a family meal! Along the lines of creativity, we have some friends with older kids who have found that dinnertime is very difficult to coordinate, so they share breakfast together several times a week.

3. Have Fun.
Finally, once we've set realistic goals and found creative ways to make them work, moms and dads have to make

mealtime something to look forward to. Making mealtimes fun might be the most important step in creating a habit that lasts.

One easy route to a fun meal is playing a mealtime game. Work on a puzzle or play a game during dinner. Kids – and especially teenagers - tend to open up and talk more when something else is going on.

Put a brainteaser, riddle, or word of the day in the middle of the table. Whoever solves the puzzle first is excused from dinner clean up. One mom puts a picture of a famous person (Ben Franklin, Martin Luther, or Booker T. Washington, for example) on the table and has her kids take guesses at who it is.

Choose a book that the whole family will enjoy and renew the forgotten tradition of reading aloud to your kids. Author Jim Trelease believes no one is ever too old to be read to. Each person can take a turn reading a chapter after dinner, even while others are cleaning up if you are really pressed for time.

For older children, you may bring the newspaper to the table and discuss aspects of an intriguing story.

A 1996 study by Dr. Catherine Shaw, Professor Of Education at Harvard University followed 65 families over an 8-year period. Guess what she found? Dinnertime was of more value to child development than playtime, school, and story time.

There is no reason that mealtimes cannot be a highlight of your day. Part of effective time management is building in time for positive, lasting memories. You have the opportunity this week to build these simple elements into your schedule. In doing so, you may do something that is life-changing!

Jump-Start Checklist: Ten Steps to Being Ready When Opportunity Knocks

1. List all of the areas in your life that affect you but over which you have no control. Ask God how you might gain more influence in that area of life.
2. Read at least one book a month pertaining to current events.
3. Review family-related news daily.
4. Make good habits more convenient. For example, if you are developing a daily Bible reading habit first thing in the morning, place your Bible right by your bed where it will be in sight when you first wake up.
5. Mark opportunities for milestones on the calendar for the next two years (birthdays, graduations, anniversaries, etc.)
6. List all of the people with whom you have an influence and then list at least one way you can serve them in a positive manner.
7. Identify the points of frustration in your life and list ways that you might adapt your lifestyle to minimize those distractions.
8. Make a list of things you have learned from the trials you have already been through, and the aspects of your life that may be stronger because of those difficult times. Use that encouragement to press forward in current struggles.
9. Seal off blocks of time on your schedule that will make you available to loved ones.
10. Identify the people in your life that make you angry or frustrated, and anticipate better ways to respond next you begin to feel this way.

Week Four Checklist:	S	M	T	W	Th	F	S
God Goals							
Scripture Memory Work	❏	❏	❏	❏	❏	❏	❏
Daily Focus (Prayer and Study) Time	❏	❏	❏	❏	❏	❏	❏
Personal Goals_____	❏	❏	❏	❏	❏	❏	❏
People Goals							
Encourage One Person	❏	❏	❏	❏	❏	❏	❏
Personal Goals_____	❏	❏	❏	❏	❏	❏	❏
Mind Goals							
Gained Wisdom through Reading, Audio Message, etc.	❏	❏	❏	❏	❏	❏	❏
Personal Goals_____	❏	❏	❏	❏	❏	❏	❏
Body Goals							
Healthy Eating Habits	❏	❏	❏	❏	❏	❏	❏
Personal Goals_____	❏	❏	❏	❏	❏	❏	❏

Week One Notes and Observations:

_____
_____
_____
_____
_____
_____
_____
_____
_____
_____
_____

Week Five: Living With Purpose

Secrets to Success: Setting Family Goals

A healthy family has healthy goals and a strong sense of direction. How can we improve our marriages? What do we want to impart on our children - or grandchildren - before they're grown? As we start off a brand new year, I want to share some practical steps for reaching family goals.

Most of us have made New Year's resolutions once or twice in our lives. We made plans to improve in some way over the coming twelve months. Unfortunately, most of these goals were forgotten by Valentines Day. When it comes to our families, goals tend to fizzle out over time.

Goal setting is normally something that is more associated with the corporate world than family life. At work, a person can make it his or her goal to increase sales by 20% - a very clear mark to reach for. At home, it's much harder to say you plan to increase quality time by 20%. Expecting quantitative results when it comes to the home front can seem much more difficult.

But the truth is you can - and I believe you must in order to see real progress - set quantifiable goals. Family members CAN choose to have dinner together three nights a week and spouses CAN choose to have at least one date without the kids each month. Single professionals possibly have the most pressure to neglect personal goals, because there is no immediate negative consequence. A lack of personal goals for anyone, however, can have lasting negative results.

Once you have made a commitment to family goal-setting, four steps can help insure a positive result:

1. **Visualize Victory.** Some would say that because most families don't have specific goals in mind, they apparently don't care enough about success and failure. I would argue that many families simply don't know where to begin. They've never settled on what a fulfilled family would look like to them. The first question every person needs to ask is, "What would make my a home a more pleasant place to live, and how can I make it better for the future?" I think every parent, for example, ought to know the five things that they want their children to remember forever. These aspects should be the focal point of parenting goals.
2. **Consider Action Steps.** The next question involves your goal - "What is the logical first step toward making that happen?" Then go out and do it. David Allen says that "Most people have a resistance to initiating a burst of energy that it will take to clarify the real meaning, for them, of something they have let in their world, and to decide what they need to do about it."
3. **Focus on What You Can Change.** Setting goals that depend in depth on what others do can leave you frustrated. Focus on actions that you can make happen. Oftentimes others will follow suit, but few do well when pushed out front.
4. **Remember the Size of the God You Serve!** Even though we want to focus on goals that we can participate in accomplishing (otherwise, we are setting other people's goals!), we need to figure in a "God-factor." By dreaming big, we recognize the power of our God to do more than we can do on our own, and we will rely on Him to get us to those goals.

"The end of wisdom is to dream high enough not to lose the dream in the seeking of it." - Author Unknown.

Jump-Start Checklist: Eight Great Tips to Getting Hold of Lifetime Goals

1. Write a short, concise mission statement that outlines your purpose in life. Include your family mission statement in this as well.
2. Brainstorm everything that you want to do in life, given unlimited time and resources. Write it down! Save the list!
3. Write down a compelling reason that you should become a better manager of your time and life. Keep this close by to motivate you as you write down your goals.
4. Start with goals that are simple and general rather than specific: "I want to raise well-adjusted children."
5. Remember that your job at first is not to identify *how* to get what you want, but simply to identify *what* you want.
6. Be sure that your lifetime goals encompass every aspect of life, and not just one narrow area. Be sure to include work, family, health, friends, finances, wisdom, and spiritual goals.
7. Remember the goal quadrant, and update it every six weeks at a minimum. Without working on all four areas at once, you are going to lag behind in all areas. Imagine your goal quadrant as the four ingredients necessary to make a recipe. If you leave one out, it can ruin the whole batch!
8. Visualize your life in ten years. Write down what you hope to be doing in the present tense: "My wife and I are enjoying new ministry opportunities in the empty nest, and our daughters have grown up to be strong, graceful Christian leaders. We have saved for just this time, and are able to travel more and really enjoy one another."

Week Five Checklist:	S	M	T	W	Th	F	S
God Goals							
Scripture Memory Work	❏	❏	❏	❏	❏	❏	❏
Daily Focus (Prayer and Study) Time	❏	❏	❏	❏	❏	❏	❏
Personal Goals_____	❏	❏	❏	❏	❏	❏	❏
People Goals							
Encourage One Person	❏	❏	❏	❏	❏	❏	❏
Personal Goals_____	❏	❏	❏	❏	❏	❏	❏
Mind Goals							
Gained Wisdom through Reading, Audio Message, etc.	❏	❏	❏	❏	❏	❏	❏
Personal Goals_____	❏	❏	❏	❏	❏	❏	❏
Body Goals							
Healthy Eating Habits	❏	❏	❏	❏	❏	❏	❏
Personal Goals_____	❏	❏	❏	❏	❏	❏	❏

Week One Notes and Observations:

_____
_____
_____
_____
_____
_____
_____
_____
_____
_____
_____

Secrets to Success: Living a Legacy

The sixth chapter of Deuteronomy is a great send-off challenge for us as we move beyond *The First Forty Days*. Verses six through nine of this dynamic chapter demonstrate to the families of Israel how to impart their values on the next generation:

"And these words which I command you today shall be in your heart. You shall teach them diligently to your children, and shall talk of them when you sit in your house, when you walk by the way, when you lie down, and when you rise up. You shall bind them as a sign on your hand, and they shall be as frontlets between your eyes. You shall write them on the doorposts of your house and on your gates."(NKJV)

In other words, the principles of God should not just become a once-per-week discussion with our kids, or a once-per-day time slot of Bible reading. God's precepts should surround everything we do. This passage also makes clear that the imparting of these principles is a **very intentional act. It does not happen by accident!** You won't become a stronger person by just setting goals, and you won't become a better parent by hoping your children turn out okay.

As we look at our passage again, we see three key reasons why *intentional action* should be our priority in establishing a life of family devotion:

***Doing* Leads to *Talking*:** Most kids talk more when they are "doing". When we find ways to stimulate communication in every day events, we open the door to share the foundations of our faith. Back in Deuteronomy 6, we notice that the Bible doesn't just say to READ the commandments throughout the day. It says to TALK ABOUT the commandments throughout the day!

***Repetition* Leads to *Legacy*:** There is something about repetition that makes things last. God's children knew this well, and used it effectively to pass along God's timeless principles. The fact of the matter is that developing core values into positive habits is the best way to turn a value into a family legacy.

***Seeing* Leads to *Believing*:** The power of association is the heart of any effective memorization tool. In all of our lives, key visual events associate themselves with the activities, thoughts, or things surrounding those events. Some are so powerful that we cannot remember one without the other. God, of course, had this figured out long before any memory expert.

You and I are called by God to create a family uniqueness just as permanent and special in our home lives. We are responsible to influence the next generation in a profound and positive way.

As we conclude our forty days together, it is essential that our words become action. Our dreams have been transformed into tangible goals. Our responsibilities have been organized into realistic tasks. Now it is time to transform our long-term goals into short-term realities, and put them into action.

And that is where the heart of true success lies: in the actions that declare our beliefs. Those actions will determine the legacy that we leave. We must choose to live as such an example that we paint an indelible picture in the minds of our children – and more importantly, in their hearts.

Jump-Start Checklist: Six Sure-Fire Steps to Short-Term Goals

1. Sometimes trying to work on all of your long-term goals in a certain period of time is overwhelming. Don't be afraid to focus on one or two long-term goals during a six-month period.

2. Begin turning your long-term goals into specific activities and placing them on the calendar. In doing so, you are actually building your short-term goals: "For the next six months, I will exercise three times per week for at least one half hour."

3. Revise your long-term goals at least once per year. Changes in your life as well as the world around you may require you to respond by adapting your goals.

4. Be sure that your goals are not dominated by activity goals. Include both attitude and spiritual goals as well. They may not be as measurable, but they are just as important if not more so. For example, seeking to become a better encourager by paying at least one sincere compliment a day is a worthwhile and attainable goal.

5. Make any organizational adjustments that will enable you to accomplish your new goals. If you have created an orderly space to conduct your focus time, you are far more likely to follow through.

6. Eliminate any unnecessary tasks from your schedule that may hinder your goals. This may be the most painful step, but it will go a long way toward ensuring success. Remember that saying yes to one task usually means saying no to another one. What do you really want to say yes to?

Week Six Checklist:	S	M	T	W	Th
God Goals					
Scripture Memory Work	❏	❏	❏	❏	❏
Daily Focus (Prayer and Study) Time	❏	❏	❏	❏	❏
Personal Goals_____	❏	❏	❏	❏	❏
People Goals					
Encourage One Person	❏	❏	❏	❏	❏
Personal Goals_____	❏	❏	❏	❏	❏
Mind Goals					
Gained Wisdom through Reading, Audio Message, etc.	❏	❏	❏	❏	❏
Personal Goals_____	❏	❏	❏	❏	❏
Body Goals					
Healthy Eating Habits	❏	❏	❏	❏	❏
Personal Goals_____	❏	❏	❏	❏	❏

Week One Notes and Observations:

_____
_____
_____
_____
_____
_____
_____
_____
_____
_____
_____

TIME MANAGEMENT SUMMARY

"SUPER SUMMARY"

Time management is doing the right things at the right moments.

The Power of Response:
- Awareness
- Anticipation
- Adaptation
- Tenacity

The Power of Direction:
- Identify your "Five Starters"
- Fill up the "Goal Quadrant":
    1. Mind goals
    2. Body goals
    3. God goals
    4. People Goals

a. Family – Safety and Legacy
b. Church – Service and Love
c. Community – Salt and Light

The Power of Planning:
- Three Components of Healthy Planning:
    1. A Teachable Spirit
    2. A Simple, Specific Calendar
    3. Sound Judgement

- Daily Direct Your Life Story – "Family F.I.L.M."
    - **F**amily Summit
    - **F**ocus Time
    - **I**dentify Immovables
    - **L**ist Tasks
    - **M**ap the Calendar

The Power of Action:
- STEP Out and Get Started
    - **S**chedule your first step.
    - **T**ime your task.
    - **E**mpty your excuse bucket.
    - **P**ress on.
- Three Power Tools
    - Habits
    - Forty Days
    - Family Traditions

THE BALANCED LIFE EVALUATION

"POST-BOOK INVENTORY"

This second evaluation is to be taken forty days after your completion of the Family Time Inventory. This should indicate where progress has been made, and areas where work still needs to be done.

Please answer as accurately as possible. This quiz is more a reflection of yourself than a scientific instrument. You could easily fudge the answers to make yourself feel better, but you will miss out on the opportunity to see a more detailed picture of your life. Remember – you are responding according to what you actually DO, and not how you HOPE to DO in the future. The more honest you are on these questions, the more helpful this exercise can be.

1) I accept the fact that many things in my life are out of my control.
____ 1. Almost Never
____ 2. Seldom
____ 3. Sometimes
____ 4. Most of the Time
____ 5. Almost Always

2) I operate on a personal mission statement I have formulated for my life.
____ 1. Almost Never
____ 2. Seldom
____ 3. Sometimes
____ 4. Most of the Time
____ 5. Almost Always

3) I like to have access to as much information as possible before making a decision.
____ 1. Almost Never
____ 2. Seldom
____ 3. Sometimes
____ 4. Most of the Time
____ 5. Almost Always

4) If someone followed me through an average day, he would get a clear picture of the things that matter most to me.
____ 1. Almost Never
____ 2. Seldom
____ 3. Sometimes
____ 4. Most of the Time
____ 5. Almost Always

5) When making decisions, I take into account

things around me that could affect my plans. (i.e., culture, rules, other people, etc...)
_____ 1. Almost Never
_____ 2. Seldom
_____ 3. Sometimes
_____ 4. Most of the Time
_____ 5. Almost Always

6) By keeping my priorities in mind, I am able to say no to distractions and interruptions throughout my day.
_____ 1. Almost Never
_____ 2. Seldom
_____ 3. Sometimes
_____ 4. Most of the Time
_____ 5. Almost Always

7) When pursuing a goal, I break it down into simple, logical steps.
_____ 1. Almost Never
_____ 2. Seldom
_____ 3. Sometimes
_____ 4. Most of the Time
_____ 5. Almost Always

8) I have a system for easy completion of things I must do on a regular basis, like bill paying, house chores, filing, etc., so that these tasks are more easily completed.
_____ 1. Almost Never
_____ 2. Seldom
_____ 3. Sometimes
_____ 4. Most of the Time
_____ 5. Almost Always

9) I am willing to change my plans in order to accommodate changing circumstances.
_____ 1. Almost Never
_____ 2. Seldom
_____ 3. Sometimes
_____ 4. Most of the Time
_____ 5. Almost Always

10) I avoid things that do not really matter, like television, surfing the Internet, and computer or video games.
_____ 1. Almost Never
_____ 2. Seldom
_____ 3. Sometimes
_____ 4. Most of the Time
_____ 5. Almost Always

11) I use one planning system for my daily life, whether it is a paper planner or digital handheld device.
_____ 1. Almost Never
_____ 2. Seldom
_____ 3. Sometimes
_____ 4. Most of the Time
_____ 5. Almost Always

12) My goals have been given a date of completion.
_____ 1. Almost Never
_____ 2. Seldom
_____ 3. Sometimes
_____ 4. Most of the Time
_____ 5. Almost Always

13) I am comfortable with doing what I ought to do even when I receive little or no immediate rewards in return.
   ____ 1. Almost Never
   ____ 2. Seldom
   ____ 3. Sometimes
   ____ 4. Most of the Time
   ____ 5. Almost Always

14) My short and long term goals are clearly written down.
   ____ 1. Almost Never
   ____ 2. Seldom
   ____ 3. Sometimes
   ____ 4. Most of the Time
   ____ 5. Almost Always

15) I find the information I need quickly, because my system of information storage is in order.
   ____ 1. Almost Never
   ____ 2. Seldom
   ____ 3. Sometimes
   ____ 4. Most of the Time
   ____ 5. Almost Always

16) When I begin my tasks for the day, I jump right in and get to work.
   ____ 1. Almost Never
   ____ 2. Seldom
   ____ 3. Sometimes
   ____ 4. Most of the Time
   ____ 5. Almost Always

17) I can often anticipate problems before they arise in the future.
____ 1. Almost Never
____ 2. Seldom
____ 3. Sometimes
____ 4. Most of the Time
____ 5. Almost Always

18) I review my short and long-term goals regularly.
____ 1. Almost Never
____ 2. Seldom
____ 3. Sometimes
____ 4. Most of the Time
____ 5. Almost Always

19) I am on time for my appointments and planned activities.
____ 1. Almost Never
____ 2. Seldom
____ 3. Sometimes
____ 4. Most of the Time
____ 5. Almost Always

20) I make it a point to stay physically fit and eat healthy foods.
____ 1. Almost Never
____ 2. Seldom
____ 3. Sometimes
____ 4. Most of the Time
____ 5. Almost Always

BLE SCORE SHEET 187

Transfer the answers from your Balanced Life Evaluation to the blanks below and to the left. Next, fill in the blank to the right of each answer with the same number. Finally, add up the four columns to discover your scores in each category.

Answers	R	D	P	A
1.				
2.				
3.				
4.				
5.				
6.				
7.				
8.				
9.				
10.				
11.				
12.				
13.				
14.				
15.				
16.				
17.				
18.				
19.				
20.				
(Add each column)	Response	Direction	Planning	Action
TOTALS				

The Balanced Life Evaluation is scored in four critical areas of the productivity process:

> **Response**: the ability to anticipate and respond with wisdom to the out-of-control aspects of life.
> **Direction**: the knowledge of how success will be defined in your life and that of your family, and setting the goals to get there.
> **Planning**: the organization of tasks and events to line them up with priorities and goals.
> **Action**: the demonstration of true commitment to your plans by going forward with the necessary tasks.

Out of a possible 25 points in each category, fill in the points you accumulated in each:

> Response: ____
> Direction: ____
> Planning: ____
> Action: ____

Some numbers to consider:

> A score of 0 – 7 in any category may mean that this area of your life is in desperate need of attention!

> A score of 8 – 12 in any category indicates that there is work to be done to achieve maximum productivity in this area.

> A score of 13 – 18 in any category means that you have obviously developed some positive habits in this area. Be sure that you bring

ALL of your categories up to this level, or this strength could become a weakness.

A score of 19 – 25 means that you are making a consistent effort, and places you in the company of a select few self-disciplined individuals on earth at this time. Use your strengths to make a difference for eternity!

There are two areas of interest you need to focus on with these scores.

LIFE BALANCE:

With regard to balance, you will want to imagine that each of these areas is a weight on one corner of a circle. This circle is balancing on a needle, and will stay balanced only as long as each end weighs the same. If it's out of balance at all, it will have a strong chance of toppling over in the long haul.

The weaker areas need to be improved first in order to improve balance, which will automatically improve productivity.

SCOPE:

With regard to scope, you will want to imagine that the bigger your scores, the bigger the "bulls-eye" on life's target becomes. In other words, you have a much greater chance of accomplishing what's important to you when all four areas have been enlarged.

This self-evaluation can be greatly enhanced by inputting your answers online at www.homeontime.com. Your response will be evaluated, and you can receive a chart which illustrates these important principles. This evaluation is a free service. Take advantage today!

Bring a Home On Time Conference to Your Area!

A three-and-a-half hour Home On Time Conference gives families greater control over their schedules, their priorities, and most importantly, their walks with God! The seminar is full of insights and ideas that can be put into practice immediately and make a difference. Host Ryan Rush shares timeless principles from God's Word in a fresh and exciting way on relevant topics such as:

> Improved Time Management at Home
> Identifying Time Wasters
> Establishing Family Priorities
> Family Goal Setting
> Family Challenges
> Family Devotion Ideas

Home on Time Conferences are available for limited dates right now. Contact us by phone or at our website, www.homeontime.com, and we'll send you a free Conference Info Pack today!

Home on Time
www.homeontime.com
(866) 247-0377

About the Author

Ryan Rush knows how to help families. As former Family Pastor of the historic Thomas Road Baptist Church, he speaks everywhere on simple steps for success at home. Ryan is a member of the National Association of Professional Organizers and the Director of the Family Ministries Network. The time management principles he shares offer Biblical insight and proven ideas that work on the home front.

Ryan holds a Bachelor of Science in Psychology from the University of Mary Hardin-Baylor and a Master of Religious Education from Christian Bible College. His radio program, *The Life and Family Show,* airs weekly in Central Virginia, and his television news segment, *The Home On Time Commentary,* is broadcast in the same region on WSET-TV.

Ryan and his wife Lana have two daughters – Ryley Anne and Reagan Anne. They live in the rugged and beautiful hill country outside of Austin, Texas.